WHAT'S NEXT AFTER ADVERTISING?

STORYTiZiNG

BOB PEARSON
Author of PreCommerce

STORYTIZING
WHAT'S NEXT AFTER ADVERTISING?

Bob Pearson with Dan Zehr

ISBN: 978-0-692-59814-6
Copyright © 2019 by 1845 Publishing

Cover and interior design by TLC Graphics, www.TLCGraphics.com.
Cover: Monica Thomas / Interior: Kimberly Sagmiller

Printed in the United States of America.

To Leo Didur, a proud
American who emigrated
from Ukraine — you were
more than a wonderful
grandfather, you were
also the first writer in our
family who inspired all of
us to "create." The book
you wrote that was never
published now comes alive
in all of our writings.

TABLE OF CONTENTS

ALL MODELS EVOLVE

> *"Yesterday's home runs don't win today's games."*
>
> **– Babe Ruth**

I f the great George Herman Ruth were around today, baseball's evolution would blow him away. Players study themselves on video to understand the minutiae of biomechanics. Statisticians predict where batted balls will go, and managers adjust their fielder's positioning for each batter. Fans watch or listen to their favorite teams on their phones. You can even buy sushi and craft beer at some ballparks. I doubt The Babe would care much for sushi in the dugout, but he'd certainly enjoy the beer. He'd also recognize the advances in today's game.

In business as in baseball, models evolve. Advertising put up a tremendous run, but the ideas that once worked wonders can often fail to make a meaningful impression today. It's not a factor of waning imagination or a lack of brilliant professionals. The industry produces some of the best and brightest marketers we meet. Rather, the way companies converse with customers has undergone a subtler—yet more fundamental—transformation as advances in technology, science and culture pushed the marketplace forward. And those changes can have deeply personal consequences for the people and the businesses that don't recognize and embrace the change.

Unfortunately, companies and professionals rarely handle change well. Back in the mid-1990s, few people could have predicted that mobile phones and tablets would drive the personal computing industry today. Back in 1980, no one could imagine water, for a couple dollars a bottle, would outsell soda. A luxury electric car for $75,000—a fantasy even just a decade ago—yet here we are with all the automakers chasing Tesla. These marketplace shifts look blatantly obvious and almost organic as time passes, but at the time we missed the key evolution because we only looked for clues on the surface.

Change rarely follows an obvious pattern. The earth's tectonic plates constantly shift beneath us, but we rarely register anything other than stillness and solidity in the ground under our feet. Only at the edges of these plates do we realize—usually with an all too stunning a jolt—that a steady motion is building more transformative pressure and friction with each passing moment. We often think of marketing, communications and sales models with the same static mindset. We've been doing this for years, and while we tweak things here and there to push the envelope just a little bit more, we rest easy in the idea that the overarching model still works pretty darn well. We're getting the results we need, maybe even a fair number of upside surprises from time to time. So why change?

We change because business models aren't earthquakes. Science can't accurately predict tremors yet, but we can identify the underlying historical forces that transform products and processes—if we know what to seek and accept the challenge of finding it. For example, advances in technology, science and culture often align to hint at what's ahead, and they guide these evolutions in remarkably consistent ways. If science changes rapidly but technology and culture lag, we don't experience the benefit of those advances. Only when all three evolve and reinforce one another do we start to realize what's really occurring under the curtain of everyday life.

Today, we stand at this tipping point in our communications and marketing worlds. Technology now allows us to identify what any customer or consumer or citizen is doing online anywhere in the world. This gives a marketing professional an unprecedented opportunity to define his or her audience and what they care about. Meanwhile, the blistering pace of new development across a range of social media allow companies to interact with customers in new and more meaningful ways.

Scientific innovation is exploding across a range of industries, particularly healthcare, where advances in research have given us a keener understanding of how doctors deliver care to patients. Physicians can now use biodegradable microchips to help inform their diagnoses and treatment options. Studies into the delivery of care have helped schools more effectively reach and teach medical students. It often takes a very long time to happen, but industries from biomedicine to entertainment to automobile design have leveraged scientific breakthroughs to transform their business models and processes.

Cultural change can take a more amorphous form, because it involves people changing their habits rather than a specific piece of software we can point to. Yet for the same reason, an evolving culture usually has the deepest impact on business and marketing. We can now Snapchat, tweet, text or live stream our daily thoughts to the customers we want to reach, and they can respond in real time. Meanwhile, the entire online audience, not just the producers of content, has the power to influence others and make a difference.

That shifting power base starts to warp the framework of the 1/9/90 model. In that construct, we long understood the critical role of the 1% who created the content we all read. They would influence the 9%, who in turn would share, shape and extend the message and the market. But how that effect would spread to the 9 percent—and from there to the 90%—the lurk-and-learn consumers—was always more of a mystery. A message still moves in mysterious ways, but we can plainly see the twist in the model. Today, the 9% carry the biggest megaphone. The five targeted personas become a figment of our quaint, past imagination. A database of five million people is outdated when you and the 9 percent can easily reach 25 million, even 250 million, consumers wherever they "live online."

We have shifted from the PESO world (paid, earned, shared and owned), where paid media carried the power. Now earned (free), shared (social media channels) and owned media wield the greatest influence on the market. Paid media remain useful catalysts to stimulate or enhance the rest, but the hierarchy of influence among them has shifted 180 degrees. This puts us on the front edge of a largely unrealized tectonic shift—where the ESO drives the P, so to speak—and marketing professionals have to rethink the way they influence the consumers and citizens of the world.

As I lay out in detail through this book, we as marketing professionals must become experts at what we call "audience architecture," so we can align our message with our customers. We will become practitioners of a radically new form of message delivery—Storytizing—where we deploy a series of models and strategies that help craft, transmit and maintain a full brand narrative to customers anywhere, anytime. But look, it's going to be a bumpy ride. Some traditional models will become obsolete, while others will adapt to the new reality. Some companies will embarrass themselves. Others will participate, but their efforts will be largely overlooked. But for those companies who work hard to study and understand the direction of the world's technological, scientific and cultural shifts, spreading a beneficial brand message will become easier. They'll optimize their marketing budgets, and their consumers will benefit.

All of this is happening today. As with my previous book in 2011, *PreCommerce*, the following chapters won't present a useless theoretical projection of what's to come a decade down the road. But also like *PreCommerce*, the observations and predictions of which are still borne out today, we'll look ahead to how this will become mainstream in the next three to four years. We see the shifts in our own firm, and with the world's most innovative marketing professionals, with whom we work. You'll find many of their stories and observations throughout.

So sit back, maybe grab a little sushi or a beer of your choice (the Babe would approve), and let's take a look beneath the surface. Let's understand the coming transformation in all its glory.

SECTION I

STORYTIZING AND AUDIENCE ARCHITECTURE

Chapter 1

FROM ADVERTISING TO STORYTIZING

*"The conventional
wisdom is
often wrong."*

– Steven D. Levitt, **Freakonomics**

When someone's on to something big, you can see it in their eyes. Greg Matthews and Matt Hager wore the look when they approached me in August 2012 and asked if I could listen to them whiteboard a new idea, so I immediately dropped what I was working on and followed them into our Longhorn conference room. Greg began to explain: He and Matt believed they'd found a way to index virtually every medical provider in the country and identify them with 100 percent accuracy by linking the provider, their social profile and registration information. As he continued, I started to realize they'd come up with the world's first custom search engine for medical providers—from doctors to pharmacists, nurses to patient advocates. They estimated a field of three million providers in the U.S. alone, but this could scale anywhere we could tie together a social profile and an official professional registration. And it could work for any industry that had registration requirements; healthcare was just the start.

Fifteen minutes into their explanation, I told Greg and Matt they'd just developed a breakthrough idea. They'd sensed they found something big, but this could become its own company or business segment. The whiteboard contained nothing more than a handful of words and some exploratory software code, but the breakthrough was as obvious as the eureka looks on their faces.

> We needed to cut out all of the noise, know exactly what a person cared about, who they followed and respected, what type of media they preferred and how we could build an appropriate and deep relationship.

The idea resonated so deeply because our team had obsessed for more than a year about the limits of traditional search. Google is wonderful, but it is so broad we couldn't identify the exact audience for a topic or profession. We needed to cut out all of the noise, know exactly what a person cared about, who they followed and respected, what type of media they preferred and how we could build an appropriate and deep relationship. We thought of it as building a "custom search engine," since it would be completely audience driven and truly custom to the profession we were tracking. And now we had our epiphany.

No one can successfully transform communications, marketing or digital-media models without knowing precisely what their audience is doing—you need the right Audience Architecture.

THE FIVE THEMES OF MARKET NEED

Like all of our ideas, the idea of audience architecture—the model that allows us to define and understand our audience—emerged from our constant study of the unmet needs in the market. Everything we do begins with this, because innovation derives from the unmet needs. If you can't prove these before you innovate, you're likely wasting your time. Sometimes those unmet needs are obvious. Sometimes the marketplace only hints at them. But they're discoverable for those who take time to look and listen.

At W2O, we listen closely when our clients debate methods to improve digital marketing. The ideas stretch far and wide, but the discussions always revolve around five common themes:

#1: SEGMENTATION IS NOT EFFECTIVE. No marketing professional ever believed that creating five personas for a brand could provide a truly accurate picture of millions of customers. One persona represented hundreds of thousands, even millions, of unique customers. We could get the high-level trends right, but to more accurately reach consumers in a PreCommerce world where they could find precisely what they needed, we have to move to a world where five personas becomes 500 or 5,000 micro-segments. We never could find the optimal segmentation because we didn't really know what most of our customers were really doing. Micro-segments, on the other hand, have few limits on how detailed a segment they can identify.

#2: PRIMARY RESEARCH IS HARDER TO DO IN TODAY'S SOCIAL WORLD. If your audience is continually shifting as they interact with and learn from their peer group, how do you know if today's primary research is still accurate tomorrow? Is there anything better than directly watching and learning from the exact customers you care about, especially when you compare that to an "n" of 1,000 that you only track quarterly? We know that primary research will continue to be important, but understanding the dynamics of subconscious behavior and primary research, which often taps short term memory, will become increasingly relevant from here on out. A combination of the two, primary and subconscious, would change the game.

#3: PAID MEDIA MUST BE OPTIMIZED TO SPEND MORE ON EARNED, SHARED AND OWNED MEDIA. Brands who spend big bucks on Internet advertising know full well that 20 to 40 percent of their spend is inefficient, could be misappropriated or is otherwise wasted. We know if we can track the right audience for a brand, that audience will tell us where and how to reach them. This alone would optimize marketing spend tremendously.

#4: EMAILING CUSTOMERS IS NOT AN EFFECTIVE WAY TO REACH PEOPLE. It's not rocket science: Reaching just 0.05% of our audience each time is a waste of money and resources. Companies are weary of the associated costs of housing all that data, throwing money at email campaigns and never quite knowing if they got any smarter about how to target their customers. We know that conversion would go way up if we knew how to better match the brand's desire to communicate with the audience's unmet needs.

#5: TRENDS ARE BEING MISSED, CAMPAIGNS ARE TOO SLOW AND OUR SPEED HAS TO CHANGE. A content cycle for a topic or brand can move at a speed measured in hours, even minutes. Campaigns that take six to nine months to build no longer work in the day-to-day shaping and reshaping of the market. They might still work for launches, but most of our effort goes into products already on the market. Even big campaigns need to adjust the campaign continually as the launch date approaches, based on the market's changing needs.

Understanding these themes provide us a platform we can use to guide our research, planning and implementation. But they also underscore the increasingly vital importance of speed and agility. For a while now, we've called paid media "dumb media" because it doesn't inform us. Today's need for speed and agility shift the premium to earned, shared and owned media because they tell us exactly what customers care about in real-time—which can be used to make that dumb media a little smarter.

> One immutable truth stands at the core of all our findings: Human beings gravitate toward the products and services that make their lives simple.

So our teams at W2O have thrown their energies into research on earned, shared and owned media, and how we can use it to increase our speed and agility. We've created algorithms for clients that work in 20 different languages to gain a better understanding of how people behave online. We already knew how to identify key influencers, what content people prefer and where they tend to go as they kick around the Web. So now we want to know what fundamental truths we can glean from nine years of conducting more than 3,000 assignments around the world—and theorize about how the lessons learned might influence a future model.

One immutable truth stands at the core of all our findings: Human beings gravitate toward the products and services that make their lives simple. No matter how crazy the outside world appears, we try to make it feel smaller and more comfortable. It seems obvious enough, but the implications for marketing are profound. I didn't realize how profound until we started theorizing about how unmet needs and the consumer's urge to simplify might influence advertising in an always-on and interactive world.

Suddenly, the current advertising models looked downright prehistoric. The market was hinting at something new, its major trends hinting at what would eventually become Storytizing.

THE PRIMAL FORCES OF THE DIGITAL WORLD

We know from working with Jeff Arnold, founder of WebMD and Sharecare, that a community of consumers can only think of approximately 200 to 500 questions about any particular malady. We mistakenly believe there are millions of healthcare questions out there, but in fact they're all rooted in a relatively finite set of queries. We know from reading the work of Dr. Vincent Covello, director of the Center for Risk Communications, that journalists ask the same 77 questions for issues over and over again. And we know from our work at W2O that fewer than 50 people create and drive the majority of content for any particular market; that a relatively limited number of people pick it up and share it; and that through that small set of people it will reach most of the market.

Who we follow and hang out with matters a great deal. We learn from each other. Most of the ideas that implant themselves in our brains come from peers, and we often grow hotter or colder on those ideas as the tenor of our online conversations change. Researching the changing shape of these interactions led us to the primal forces in today's market, forces that act subtly on an everyday personal basis but exert a major influence on our digital world.

We make the world finite

We act more like a herd than we realize. We really find more comfort when conforming to our communities, whether we believe it or not.

We always fall into habits and patterns

We go to the same channels, listen to the same people and rarely change much unless our herd does so. It's why Facebook never felt much pressure from Google+. Everyone would go to Google+ if all your friends moved there, but they didn't.

How we learn is evolving

We are learning faster and more frequently from social media and search than we are from mainstream outlets. This profoundly changes how we think and act.

What we really want is not always what we say

We vote on what is important everyday by what we search, view, download, share and like. If you ask a direct question, we'll tell you an answer, but our actions will always speak louder (and more accurately) than our words.

THE SHIFT TO STORYTIZING

The primal forces that shape consumer behavior and brand perceptions today have flipped the advertising model on its head. In the past, the top-down advertising model, designed to gain our attention and then convince us to act, helped shape even online behavior. People often moved to new sites and services with an effective nudge from an ad. Remember all those over-the-top, multimillion-dollar commercials during Super Bowls past? They still can work when deployed in the right environment, but it's really the grassroots, bottom-up approach that drives consumer behavior today. Our customers want to learn in their channel of choice, from the community trusted in that channel. They want to receive the full story on a brand, subject or issue—for better or worse—they don't want to go searching far and wide for it. They want customized information based on their ever-changing needs. And while they might never articulate those needs, they will tell us by what they touch, spend time on, click and share.

Storytizing refers to a brand's ability to make its full story accessible to a present or future customer at anytime, anywhere in the world, and based on the needs of the customer.

This 180-degree shift to a bottoms-up approach will force a 180-degree shift in marketing models as well. It requires a transition from the traditional, advertising-driven marketing strategy to one that tells a never-ending, holistic, constantly evolving story. It requires Storytizing.

Storytizing refers to a brand's ability to make its full story accessible to a present or future customer at anytime, anywhere in the world, and based on the needs of the customer. If a customer can receive and access the full story, or at least the part relevant to them, and if they can access it in their preferred channel at their preferred time, the message starts to become truly relevant to their needs.

To effectively Storytize, then, we must learn from our audience directly, based on what they do across earned, shared and owned media. Depending on what they tell us via their actions, we can determine how to build the right relationship, which forms of media are most effective, who has the most influence, what time of day is best and any number of other factors that will allow us to better align our story with our customers' needs. We can't do any of this without developing an effective Audience Architecture to fully understand the needs of our customers. And we need to gauge the proper Audience Alignment to ensure that what we do is what our customers will appreciate and respect in the short-, mid- and long-term.

In its most simple terms, Storytizing is the opposite of advertising. Advertising develops an idea or campaign and pays to put it in front of an audience. Storytizing starts by listening directly to customers, and then it curates their ideas or develops new ideas to satisfy the unmet needs of the audience.

TOWARD A BETTER AUDIENCE ARCHITECTURE

Greg and Matt left the Longhorn conference room and went back to their normal work at our firm, but they knew they'd developed a new hobby that, soon enough, would become their full time job. But they still had to crack an extremely difficult problem, one that had prevented many firms before us from a fully effective method to track an online audience. We would need to build software that could match up a variety of databases with registration information, social information and disparate data sets, such as Medicare and Medicaid claims.

> We went from performing crude surgery in the dark to turning on the operating room lights and making precise cuts.

That's when we remembered Cary Jardin, one of the most brilliant software developers we know. Cary has written several books on Java technology, holds ten patents and created the entire Java infrastructure attached to enterprise online transaction processing (OLTP) systems at NCR. As much as anyone, Cary has shaped Java, a programming language that runs on more than three billion devices today. He's a problem solver of the highest level—a genius in our minds—so we called him. Fortunately for us, he agreed to help us solve the problem, and in less than six months we made enough progress to convince us we could crack this nut.

With Cary's developments in place, we started adding providers and their social profiles in a methodical manner, and soon enough we had a custom search engine that could show users what every cardiologist, nurse or other practitioner in a specific field was doing online. We called it MDigitalLife, and it was an eye-opener. Where once our lack of detailed knowledge about a client's audience would frustrate and limit our efforts to improve and optimize their marketing mix, now we generate a much more detailed view of their customer's online behavior. We went from performing crude surgery in the dark to turning on the operating room lights and making precise cuts.

We could now act as our own architect and define the audiences that our clients care about. We no longer had to make educated guesses about customer behavior. We could get a higher-definition picture of their online activity and do it in all but real time. We now had the Audience Architecture, and we could use it to match our clients' messages with their customers' needs. And it hit me: the new Madison Avenue wasn't on Main Street, as we so long assumed. The new Madison Avenue was on My Street.

WHAT WAS COMPLEX IS SIMPLE AGAIN

Leonardo da Vinci once said that "simplicity is the ultimate sophistication." Steve Jobs believed much the same: "Simple can be harder than complex. You have to work hard to get your thinking clean to make it simple. But it's worth it in the end because once you get there, you can move mountains." At W2O, we know we're on to something when the model gets simple. The digital marketing world had started to feel busier, noisier and more cluttered. But as we tinkered and upgraded MDigitalLife, I realized we had a machine that could help slow it back down.

The idea of Storytizing and Audience Architecture made the complex simple again. Successful brands will become experts in Audience Architecture. And once they accomplish that, they will start to provide the most relevant and full story to their current and future customers. They will Storytize.

HOW AN AUDIENCE'S POWER IS DISCOVERED

By Greg Matthews, managing director of MDigitalLife.
Greg was previously director of consumer innovation for Humana, he has worked in
Human Resources for Braun Consulting and is a life-long Chicago Cubs fan.

Like so many big ideas, MDigitalLife was conceived in the summer of 2012, when Matt Hager and I were both working late on our own projects and struck up a conversation as a way to take a break from our labors.

At the time, I'd spent two years at the W2O Group focusing on helping our health-care clients make better marketing and communications decisions based on social analytics. And while our brilliant analysts rarely failed to dazzle them, I kept hearing, "This is amazing – but can you tell me more about the doctors?" At that time I was already following a list of about 3,000 doctors on Twitter, so it wasn't hard to *listen* to what doctors were saying, but it was pretty tough to *analyze* it. And analyzing it was important. What we saw anecdotally was that these online doctors were beginning to fundamentally reshape the way people were thinking and talking about health. If we could help our clients – and the doctors themselves – quantify and understand those changing patterns, it could be an incredibly valuable contribution to the health of people around the world.

What our clients were asking for wasn't as simple as asking to see more conversations from doctors. They wanted to know more about the online doctors themselves – what they were doing and why. It wouldn't do to just analyze what they were saying about a topic or two.

- INSIGHT: *Essentially, I needed to perform a never-ending digital ethnographic study, looking at everything doctors do and say online, where they say it and who they say it to.*

One of the shortcomings of social media analysis from an audience perspective is that different people tell you different things about who they are. Some will be really specific – "I'm Bob Johnson, M.D. I am an interventional cardiologist at Johns Hopkins in Baltimore, Maryland." Others will be far more vague. If you're trying to give insights about an *audience*, vagueness just won't do, especially since our clients were typically focused on a single physician specialty (e.g., cardiology) in a specific geographic region (e.g., the southeastern United States). When Matt Hager came back to me a day or two later having discovered that we could freely access the official registry of every healthcare professional in the U.S. – containing their exact name, all specialties in which they were qualified to practice, and the street address of their practice – I knew we'd struck gold.

- INSIGHT: *Access to an independently verified data source completely changes the level of precision we can use to study an audience's online behavior.*

As we worked with the data over time, we recognized something else, too. Finding audiences online is actually easy. But the precision analysis we were suddenly able to do with physicians wasn't because we'd cataloged a bunch of doctors' digital footprints; it was because the data was organized and structured in such detailed ways that we could literally unearth insights that nobody else in the world could. The government database we used made that easy for U.S. doctors. But as we started indexing other populations for which no corresponding list existed (e.g., patients, advocacy organizations or doctors practicing in other countries), we found that we could gain the same benefit by creating our own set of taxonomies – or attributes – for each audience.

- INSIGHT: *Building a digital audience is easy. Appending the right metadata to each audience member to allow us to do detailed analysis and purposeful Audience Architecture is hard - but it is both possible and absolutely essential.*

Chapter 2

AUDIENCE ARCHITECTURE

*"Society is always
taken by surprise
at any new example
of common sense."*

- Ralph Waldo Emerson

urprises arise from the same fundamental condition—when events deviate from our expected set of rules and norms. But different surprises spark drastically different reactions. There's the haunted house scream and soil your underpants variety. There's the unimagined upset in sports, when the David slays the Goliath. And then there's the more mundane, everyday things that, as C+C Music Factory once noted, make you go hmmm. Business surprises tend to live on the low-intensity end of that spectrum, and they usually travel in packs. When we witness the emergence of a new model, we can see it in the hesitation people have when the evolution affects their work. It lives in the questions they ask to clarify what's happening, and it lingers in the way they can't stop thinking about an idea long after confronting it. The surprise doesn't come as a jolt, but a gentle nudged awakening to the fact that, once again, there's a better way.

To help us process these surprises better and faster, W2O lives by an innovation standard that we call the "Rule of Three." When we have a new concept we're kicking around, we need to have at least three clients say "This is important, I need this" before we will move forward. We instituted the rule because it helps us judge both the novelty and the usefulness of a surprising concept. In essence, it shows whether we're taking the right path and, if so, the idea becomes one we're "obsessed with." We know we have something, now we need to figure out how big it can become.

In many cases, it takes months to reach our Rule of Three threshold, but on occasion an idea moves much, much quicker—and the surprise comes as more of a jolt than a nudge. That was how I felt listening to Seth Duncan in a Warner Brothers conference room. We'd co-hosted an innovation session at the studio's offices in Burbank, Calif., and were joined by representatives from Warner Bros., Whole Foods, Nike, Verizon, Clarabridge and Sysomos. Duncan was explaining a new concept he called Socialgraphics. He, Paul Dyer and Andy Boothe had worked with our analytics team to pioneer a new way to track the 9% of customers who shape and share a brand's message with the 90% of consumers who just lurk and learn.

> As Duncan laid out his idea of Socialgraphics, we realized we'd found the missing piece of the puzzle— Audience Architecture.

We all knew technology advances and cultural changes had unleashed the power of this 9% cohort. They redefined how an active part of the audience could shape the actions of one another and of the rest of the audience. But up until then, we had no idea how we could precisely gauge the ways an audience works and, even if we found that, how we could scale the process to work across millions of customers around the globe.

And then came the jolt. As Duncan laid out his idea of Socialgraphics, we realized we'd found the missing piece of the puzzle—Audience Architecture.

Audience Architecture provided a blueprint for how we would design and construct this new model. The plan centered on the well-established 1-9-90 model (which I mentioned in the Introduction and discuss more fully in the next chapter). For the last nine years, W2O has refined a rather intense algorithm that shows exactly who comprise the 1% that influence the market via content creation. We've found that, worldwide, there is never more than 50 people who drive the majority share of conversation in a market.

But as Duncan noted that day in Burbank, the ability of today's audiences to reshape both the brand message and their own reaction to it is largely influenced by the 9%. And now, with socialgraphics, we could see with much greater precision what that 9% were doing. The new algorithmic approach reveals who shapes a market, what they share, what they like, and whom they respect.

PIECING TOGETHER THE AUDIENCE ARCHITECTURE

Great architecture requires more than one brilliant flourish. It blends the imagination, design and erection of an entire structure that is functionally sound, aesthetically consistent with its environment and socially inspiring. It requires both a depth and breadth of coordination, and it must flex to accommodate virtually any scenario. Audience Architecture would have to work efficiently and effectively across every part of the marketing mix. It had to fit into and enrich the existing marketing puzzle. So before we just threw this into the mix, we had to look at the six other key pieces of that rapidly changing puzzle.

Our use of mobile phones is driving a shift to responsive experience

When people consume more than half their content via phones, they have to get exactly the content they want when they want it. Otherwise, they go away. Responsive design made sure all of our sites showed up well on each device. That was the critical focus a few years ago, but now it is table stakes. This is no longer adequate. Now, we need to provide what people want when they want it on the first interaction. Responsive experience now requires the urgency we once gave responsive design. We need to know our audience as well as we know our neighbors, and then provide them what they want whenever they visit our site or channel.

We want content anywhere, anytime, anyplace

If you create content, you own it and you need to make it available where the customer is hanging out. Location no longer determines where we deliver our message. Our content is liquid and ever moving. This means media planning will change, so we match up with the needs of our audience against a proposed plan that, a week from now, might not be based on the reality of the market.

When a customer visits our website, we should be ready to "shake hands" digitally

If we understand what our customers are doing and searching for before they reach our site, we know what they want when they arrive. Heck, they've explained it to us themselves—if we've been listening. Our content experience must match up and meet those needs and desires when they arrive. We can do this by creating content packages that cover a range of potential experiences, keep them invisible to the naked eye and deliver them as we know what the customer wants upon their arrival. We won't always know the answer, so we need to develop content distribution platforms that make it possible for the customer to easily and quickly select the content and experience they want.

Top social channels will become centers of commerce

Customers are forming life-long habits inside the social channels they inhabit each day. The trust today's consumer puts in the online channel mimics the trust we used to put in our corner grocer. It means that Facebook, Apple, Google, Twitter, LinkedIn and other major social channels have the ability to become our "go to" place for e-commerce. We'll still load up a shopping cart, but we'll do it through the channel of our choice. The ubiquity of e-commerce will become standard.

Word of mouth will become a science and the designated market area (DMA) will melt away

For years, advertising has relied on the population-centric DMA structure to guide media planning. Now we can start to see what people care about by town, city, state and nation. And more importantly, we can see how people and towns align across a region. So, we can see the 500-plus communities that are like-minded in 37 different states. That's far more relevant than a shotgun approach based on population.

Geo-listening can show us what matters by neighborhood

Our phones and our social profiles make it abundantly clear where we are and what we care about. With geo-listening tools and analytics, we can see what like-minded people care about at the neighborhood or event level. We can look across a broad supply chain of similar locations—say, 1,000 movie theaters—and isolate what we want to know.

THE KEY CHARACTERISTICS OF THE 9%

When we looked at those six key sections of framework in which we would set our Audience Architecture, we discarded the obvious trends. We all know people read fewer newspapers. Online advertising, particularly banner ads, are decreasing effective. We swim in the same pool of trends that you do, but acknowledging that doesn't make any of us smarter. What really matters is how our audience is *changing*, and how we build a new model that fundamentally changes how we reach our audience. We need to stop talking at our customers and start learning more from them. Only then can we tailor our game plan to meet their needs.

When we open our ears and eyes to the message the audience is sending us, the 9% segment actually becomes even *more difficult* to categorize. Influence in the 9% cannot be measured by content creation and reaction to those contributions. We have to build a representative sample of this market segmentation. If there are one million people in the 9% of our marketplace, we can track 10,000 or 50,000 who reliably represent the larger group. We've found that cohorts of this size can reveal a reliable set of key characteristics:

What content is most important and why?

We can weight all of the content they consume and figure out what topics and messages are most important. Armed with that insight, we can create relevant content with more efficiency and we can share it with the audience segments that care rather than blindly blasting it at everyone.

Who do they follow and respect?

Customers figure out how to stay relevant and get the content they need by following people they trust and respect. So who do they follow, and which of the people they follow have more power than we previously realized? We can then develop a follower strategy for the brand and start to converge our ecosystems—provided that we are cool, share good content and earn our place at the table.

What time of day are they most active on the topic we care about?

Every day for every topic, there are peak times of activity. If we align our timing with theirs, we reach our intended audience. Once we know this schedule, we can properly time our earned, shared, owned and even paid media.

What forms of media are most relevant to the audience?

Each micro-segment tends to use specific devices at specific times. Do they rely on photos, videos or text? Are they telling stories, having fun or learning something new? If we know their habits of how they use content, we know how to shape our campaign approach to make sure we offer the right forms of media, not just the right content.

Where are they located and what does that tell us?

Are they sharing and communicating only locally? Nationally? Globally? Or do their communications cut across regions in some other piecemeal pattern? If we understand the shape and boundaries of their online world, we can understand the angle to best approach them.

BUILDING THE HOUSE

If you were starting a new television show tomorrow, the six characteristics above—when properly researched and employed—could identify the guests you should feature each day, which topics the audience would embrace, and identify who and where your next 10,000 viewers are awaiting your approach. In this sense, Audience Architecture can become audience creation. But to build this new house, we need three raw materials:

1. **THE RIGHT ALGORITHMS** — You have to have algorithms that can tell you who creates content (the 1%) and who shares content (the 9%) to reach out to the lurk-and-learn 90%.

2. **A MARKET-BASED TAXONOMY SMART FILTER** — Once you precisely identify the audience's habits, you can build a market-based taxonomy that serves as a smart filter. Think of this as columns across a spreadsheet, each helping filter your audience. Your columns cover type of event, content topic, location, social channel and even individual names. You filter the world's information from all mainstream media and online channels and determine exactly what your audience cares about at any time.

3. **A CUSTOM SEARCH ENGINE PLATFORM** — Now that you know who shapes your market, you can take a representative sample of the market and index them in a custom search engine. This will show you exactly what they do and say each day in relation to your brand or topic. Of course, the larger the sample the more precise the reading. But because technological advances now allow us to gather and analyze massive datasets, there's virtually no limit to the size of the sample you deploy.

THE RIPPLE EFFECT OF AUDIENCE ARCHITECTURE

The result is an automated brain that allows you to see who matters and what your audience actually cares about. And this Audience Architecture has a ripple effect on most, if not all, the marketing and communications models we hold dear.

Market research

We can now see with much greater accuracy the subconscious behavior of an audience. We can pull a select population and use it, with repeatable statistical accuracy, for our primary research. This has never been possible before, and that lack of precision was a glaring, original flaw in social research—one often pointed out by marketing researchers who crave repeatable and reputable data. We have it now, and it tells us that consumers, as they become desensitized to partisan views in politics or heavy-handed promotional efforts, pull back on what they will reveal publicly. But even then, they never stop showing what they care about via online movements and conversations and, as a result, we now have a better way to predict trends even when consumers try to conceal them.

The PESO Model

We can now look at earned, shared and owned behavior to see what consumers really think. Earned will tell us what we care about when we're on our own. Shared tells us what consumers care about when they contribute to our brand channels. And owned tells us what they want when they need to visit us. And all of this information, accurate at the audience level, informs us about the outlets that actually matter for paid media. So the model flips, with the ESO now guiding the P. This will cut out tremendous waste. Imagine knowing which pieces of your media plan do not correlate to your audience's location and desires.

> Audiences are living, breathing communities that change due to their experience and needs.

Customer relationship management (CRM)

Current CRM systems rely on a platform or relational database that houses all information on customers, who are then targeted for emails, coupons and other forms of outreach that hope to spur a key behavior.

With Audience Architecture, you can identify the thousands or millions of audience members online and see how they act and evolve on a daily basis. Audience Architecture platforms will become complementary to existing CRM frameworks, so that we can see what the audience really thought of outreach and, perhaps most important, whether that audience of 1 million expanded to 1.2 million or contracted to 900,000—and why it grew or shrank. Audiences are living, breathing communities that change due to their experience and needs.

Search engine optimization

We can greatly refine SEO as we learn how to understand the real search needs of our community, and then start to use that knowledge to replace the limited insight we get from the less-precise, aggregate views provided by Google or Bing. What the world as a whole searches for remains important, but we really care most about the questions our target audience asks, so we can introduce the right answers in the right forms.

Creative

Our creative teams remain the most important and impactful group, but it too will have to evolve to reach audiences in new ways. Because we know what audiences care about in real-time, we can start to develop agile campaigns that introduce content just minutes or hours after we detect interest. We know that campaigns created over six to nine months are out of date by the time they launch, so we will come up with new ways to create campaign content. Instead of preparing for the big bolus injection of content (otherwise known as launch day), we'll prepare a library of content that we can select at the right moment across a continual campaign that never stops. Yes, we'll still do big launches, but we'll do them with our eye focused on the daily shaping of conversations and communities. Launches will serve as a catalyst, not the final solution.

Like all new models, though,
those who cling to the
status quo will reject
Audience Architecture,
even as those who quickly
see its simplicity and power
come to embrace it.

The inevitable move to a new Audience Architecture will deliver many surprises. Whether a nudge or a jolt, each surprise will remind us to constantly update and improve our marketing strategy. Like all new models, though, those who cling to the status quo will reject Audience Architecture, even as those who quickly see its simplicity and power come to embrace it. It's how our world works. Whether you fall into early adoption or reticent acceptance, it will help to first understand how Audience Architecture meshes with the 1-9-90 and other traditional marketing models we've long trusted. We'll look at those next.

Chapter 3

MARKETPLACE GRAVITY AND THE 1-9-90 MODEL

> *"The most important thing in communication is hearing what isn't said."*
>
> *- Peter Drucker*

G ravity is one of the primary forces of the universe. Without it, life as we know it would not exist. Except for the relatively few people who experience the absence of gravity, none of us really notice it on a day-to-day basis. We see its effects when we drop our mobile phones, but most of us *feel* it. It's just there, also doing its thing.

The online world has its own version of marketplace gravity. Marketing professionals refer to it as the 1-9-90 model, and they interact with it on a regular basis. But for the vast majority of the world's online populace, it's just there also, doing its thing. Less than 1% of a market creates new content, approximately 9% shares that content, and the other 90% lurks and learns, benefitting from the work of the creators and sharers. We've seen this model work in B2B, B2C and throughout the world with remarkable consistency. We never see more than 1% of a market create content. On occasion we'll see a larger share, up to 20%, of a market share content, but it usually sticks pretty close to the 9% guideline. The rest of us, always the overwhelming majority, we're in it for the ride.

In *PreCommerce*, my first book, I wrote extensively about the importance of influencers, who represent the 1%. Through our algorithms, we learned that you never have more than 50 people who drive the majority of content for a market. Influencers shape our conversations more than we realize and they continue to be incredibly important. Even more relevant for most brands is their diversity. They change by country, language, topic and sub-topic—even for the same brand. So we build a modern day outreach list of exactly who matters and match it up against our brand message.

> Human beings love
> to follow patterns.
> It's how we're wired.

Yet their influence is waning. Today, technology advances have sparked an explosion of power among the 9%. This middle group has shifted the market's gravitational forces. Customers might not recognize the change—marketplace gravity keeps doing its thing—but those who study the market can see how this shift redirects consumer needs and behaviors.

THE 1-9-90 MODEL

Human beings love to follow patterns. It's how we're wired. We process and store information in a linear way, which helps us remember the alphabet or a language. Because our brains tend to work in this vectored manner, an image that harkens to past experience or a trusted friend recommending something will usually trigger a distinct response from us. So, whether involuntarily or on purpose, we all end up playing a distinct role in the social media ecosystem.

In this environment, the 1% don't have to have the most money or power, as we traditionally defined it. Rather, they are the bloggers, forum posters, video reviewers and journalists who create content. They focus on telling a story and, if they do it well, they start to gain a reputation as topic experts. But they're a small few, never more than 50 who drive the majority share of conversations for a brand or topic, according to our research.

The 9% need not have money or power either, but to maintain their influence they typically need to remain highly active online. Many of you who read this book fit this category. We recommend, share, sign up, download, comment and take other actions that let our communities and our peers know how we feel about certain topics. In many respects, this group serves as a trust filter for the rest of the marketplace, which tends to believe someone who shares content brings a more objective view than the content's creator. If I tell you this book is good, you might believe me, but you'll sprinkle a grain of salt on my word. If your trusted friend or business colleague reads the book and tells you she thought it was good, you more likely believe her.

The rest of the customer base soaks it all in. They're satisfied using search or relying on the content and recommendations provided by their peers. But it's wrong to think of them as passive. The 1% might create the content and the 9% might filter it, but in the end it's everyone else who decides how compelling your brand's story really is. They go to Google, hang out on Facebook, Snapchat or another community and watch what everyone else does—but they also make decisions based on what they absorb, and that could mean success or failure for your brand.

Customers and their
friends in the marketplace
decide what will sell and
for how long.

To some extent, the PreCommerce world changed how each of the 1-9-90 influence a brand message. But in recent years, we've seen the center of marketplace gravity shift to the 9%, and they've become the people who essentially "sell" your wares. The company or content producers no longer hold all the power to make or break the product. Customers and their friends in the marketplace decide what will sell and for how long.

THE 9% IS EXPLODING DUE TO CHANNELS, TECHNOLGY NUMBER OF PEOPLE ONLINE AND RISE OF MOBILE.

UNLEASHING THE 9%

In the "old days" of social media, sharing your thoughts on someone else's work took a fair bit of savvy and effort. We could comment on blogs or add comments in a forum, but we couldn't easily and quickly share content wherever we wanted. Today, we almost take this for granted, but it didn't just happen in a vacuum. Four fundamental changes unlocked these abilities—and unleashed the power of the 9%.

1. *Real-time sharing turned us into commentators on life.* We can share photos and videos of ourselves with our friends and communities, and we can do it instantaneously through Snapchat, Instagram or WeChat. We can comment on an article and send it to anyone anywhere. This not only empowers the 9% as commentators on the news du jour, it allows them to shape the story and start their own, related conversations.

2. *We can take content and commentary from one channel and share it with the entire world.* Part of the problem in the early development

of digital media was every channel's or website's goal to capture their audience. Everyone wanted to get you to visit and then stay there, forgetting that customers want to visit and then share and interact with their peers. By finally acknowledging this mistake, thoughtful brands have made their channels even more valuable to their customers and themselves.

3. *Visual content is far easier to consume.* It used to take forever to download and view videos, so we used it sparingly and mostly through YouTube. Now, we can create, share and consume video anywhere, whether on our smart-phone apps, YouTube, Hulu or virtually any other website. And since people often prefer to learn visually, this only helps amplify a brand message (in good ways and bad).

4. *Geo-location opens up how we build our network.* The rising sophistication of geo-location and the merger of that with digital media allow users to make deeper connections on a local level. They can use this newfound connection to accelerate the expansion of their networks, rather than slowly introducing themselves to and establishing trust in an established network. If we want to find friends who like yoga in Austin, we check out #besomebody. Sure enough, we can find out who in our own apartment complex likes yoga, and we can ask them if they'd like to go to a class together.

This confluence of trends creates a much more intense form of marketplace gravity than we've seen before. The 9% are becoming the social glue that binds us. Increasingly, they influence consumer behavior and help their peers decide who and what are relevant to their world. They even have a more technical influence on the spread of messaging. For example, because they share so much content, and share it through a lens of their own thinking, they have a major impact on search engine optimization. So while years ago we'd tell our clients they needed to "join the conversation," we now advise them to align with the real decision-makers for their brand.

USING AUDIENCE ARCHITECTURE
TO LEARN FROM CUSTOMERS

The good news is that, with the 1% and 9% driving the rest, companies can become more precise in building their Audience Architecture—and glean higher quality, rather than larger quantities, of feedback.

We now can track which channels matter within the context of **the content cycle**. In other words, a story that starts on Twitter might move to Instagram and then to Facebook. Its arrival on Facebook might trigger another story, which spreads across Facebook and then back out to Twitter and other social media. Precisely tracking the 9% gives a company greater insight into the content cycle and how it shapes the brand story.

With this capability, we can stop measuring one channel and start measuring **the channel chain** for a conversation or content cycle. This will change how we focus our time on earned and shared media and impact where we place paid dollars. If the purpose of paid media is to catalyze a story, we might choose to deploy it toward the end of the cycle to keep the conversation going. Or if we use paid media to create awareness and start a conversation, we could start on one channel and quickly shift dollars when the conversation heats up elsewhere. We've learned, thus far, that chains usually encompass two to four locations but, because chains reflect the leaders' communities, don't usually go far beyond that. At the core of this, leaders are simply sharing with the communities they care about. That almost never occurs in just one arena, so we have to match our resources against the entire channel chain.

If we study the history of a market over the course of a couple years, we can start to identify which channels exert the most influence on a discussion and at what times. This has kick-started **a new form of predictive marketing** built on historical channel information. Now we study channels on a daily, weekly and monthly basis, and we can use that insight to plan, on an ongoing real-time basis, both the product launch and the post-launch support.

HARNESSING MARKETPLACE GRAVITY

The radical aspect of this gravitational pull manifests itself not in a company's efforts, but the customer's actions. Through earned, shared and owned media, the audience's actions directly inform our predictive models—and do so in real time. We can no longer look at paid media and draw conclusions on its programmatic use. That data only tells a piece of the story, and usually with just one snapshot in time. So we need to test this data against the information we glean through earned, shared and owned behavior.

> Our reputation is being shaped across multiple channels, but now we can see who is shaping it.

Our reputation is being shaped across multiple channels, but now we can see who is shaping it. We can unleash our employees, who are already online and contributing to the conversation. We can see and empower those who shape our story, giving them even more content to up their game and disseminate our story. And with the emergence of geo-location, we can dissect the 1% and the 9% even further to identify mini 1-9-90 models at the city or state level—only accelerating our ability to micro-segment our audience.

The unleashed 9% will reshape how we attract an audience and build relationships with our customers. They now reside at the very core of the marketplace's gravitational force. We don't need to account for every ounce of that force. As renowned astrophysicist Neil deGrasse Tyson notes, we can only account for about one-sixth of the force of gravity we see in the universe, yet even that fraction displays an incredible force. Marketing professionals can't know all 10 million members of their brand audience, but they can tap into the remarkable power of the 10% who shape the rest.

Like Dr. Tyson suggests, something we've never touched makes stuff move. He and his colleagues will keep searching, of course, but we don't need to know everything about gravity to appreciate it. Nor do we need to know every facet of marketplace gravity to realize its power. By tapping into power we do understand, we can influence the broader audience. But we need to show respect for gravity; it's unforgiving if we don't.

ARE YOU FUTURE READY?

By Jim Weiss, founder and CEO of W2O Group.
He worked in communications leadership positions at Genentech, Sanofi
and Heartport before starting W2O Group in his San Francisco loft in 2001.
It now employs more than 750 people in a dozen offices. Jim has worked with
The Newhouse School at Syracuse University to create the Center for Social Commerce,
a first of its kind program among colleges.

The convergence and connectivity of technology, influence and reputation impacts not only how brands and organizations break through and gain attention, but how they develop and implement new thinking and new approaches. As a result, the world is always on.

PreCommerce – as Bob outlined in his previous book – is the essential model to harness and scale influence by connecting ideas, opinions and networks that lead to advocacy and, ultimately, to the purchase. It incorporates paid, earned, shared and owned channels, tailoring the mix and message according to customer indicators and usage. *Storytizing* takes PreCommerce strategies to the next level, to more effectively inform, educate and entertain people–all in order to entice them to take complementary action via stories and narratives that capture personal interest.

As we grow W2O Group, my No. 1 goal is to ensure we remain true to our real value, which lies in the ability to ensure our clients remain *relevant in a distracted world*. And in my view, that's all about being *Future Ready*.

In our client interactions today, we start with data and analytics but move quickly into insight, strategy, content and action. The content piece, when released to the online audience, which shares and shapes it, becomes a brand's *Storytizing* in its rawest form. It's driven by a suite of proprietary analytics and insights, which we provide through a cadre of analysts and data scientists. We supplement that with our proprietary models that identify the right influencers – and those influencing the influencers – who collectively drive the majority share of conversation and dictate the narrative for any subject, product or brand.

In sum, these data and models provide companies and organizations with fresh insights and new, engaging stories that impact purchase intent and interest, as well as employee engagement and advocacy. It drives content development and creation, outreach and engagement. It enriches communications, visual storytelling and, most importantly, strategic planning.

From a business standpoint, it's about partnering with well-known brands to recalibrate their media and influencer outreach, public relations, communications and marketing planning and focus those efforts on product launches, brand enhancement, issues and crisis mitigation, customer advocacy, change management and internal communications/employee engagement – all so companies can make smarter decisions and employ more effective programming.

To deliver against this new model, identifying and nurturing talent matters most. And being Future Ready from a talent perspective means harnessing four things:

1. *Curiosity* – Always looking for the why and what's next

2. *Embracing technology* – Seeing new solutions and benefits

3. *Utilizing data and insight into planning* – Becoming savvy about analytics in uncovering opportunities

4. *Innovating fast and frequently* – Seeking out new approaches and methodologies and learning quickly

But how do you get there? You start right at the beginning. Our partnership with Syracuse University's S.I. Newhouse School of Public Communications and its W2O Center for Social Commerce facilitates invention, innovation and disruption to traditional learning methods and systems. Through the on-campus W2O Center we work closely with educators and students on developing a *Future Ready* skill set, assimilating the latest in technology and applications to deliver the next-generation workforce for our profession – one that transcends marketing, public relations/communications, creative, advertising, research, data/analytics and business strategy.

Closer to home, W2O University is our internal professional competency model, where staff, clients and outside experts conduct a variety of workshops, seminars, classes and conferences on all aspects of *PreCommerce* and *Storytizing*.

Putting these models into action requires a new mindset throughout your organization, and it begins with having a talent base ready, willing, and able to master the new reality facing business today. We must remain *Future Ready*.

Chapter 4

LEARNING FROM HISTORY

"*Those who do
not remember the
past are condemned
to repeat it.*"

- George Santayana

I'll admit it: I had to fight to stay awake in history class. I'd find some of it interesting, but I could take only so many places, dates and names before my mind would wander and I'd miss something. As my career progressed, though, I began to understand how much I'd missed by not absorbing a fuller historical context for what I was doing. And when I finally did see the deep relevance of those history lessons, I couldn't get enough of them. I've become a bit of a history nut. If I hadn't left them so exhausted, my longsuffering teachers might even be proud.

So as I started contemplating the notion that would become Storytizing, I naturally started boning up on the history of the marketing, communications and advertising professions. We cannot explain where we are and where we're going without first knowing where we've been. I went through the traditional canon, including a re-read of David

Ogilvy's classic *Ogilvy on Advertising*. I sought other works, such as Dr. Gordon Allport's 1936 study about the importance of language. I looked for as much of the current research I could find. All this study coalesced around a singular purpose—identify the old trends that remained relevant and repeatable over the decades, and then determine whether and how they might work in today's dramatically shifting marketplace.

Some remain timeless, and some well past their prime. But in the spirit of George Santayana's truism about the reasons we remember the past, it's important to note the ideas from whence the marketing profession came.

THE TIMELESS TRENDS

My informal survey of marketing history and current research convinced me that several longstanding, fundamental trends remain true today, and likely will long into the future. There are plenty more, of course, but these struck me as especially relevant in a Storytizing world.

> After all, people tend to
> embrace ideas that inspire
> us to dream of a better life.

Hope and aspiration lead us to find what's next

People started to move halfway around the world after companies placed advertisements explaining the potential of these "new" colonies. The British Empire expanded, in small part, on the marketing skills of colonial businesses. Judging from their results and the spread of Western European influence across much of the globe, they convinced a lot of people. After all, people tend to embrace ideas that inspire us to dream of a better life. We can't help but wonder whether the grass is greener on the other side.

Storytelling is central to who we are

As young boys, the campfire became one of our first attempts to share what we'd learned with our friends—and that usually came in the form of stories. Before the arrival of paper, history was most often passed down orally, through stories. The dissemination of stories only accelerated with the advent of paper and the press. The tape recorder, which came out in the 1950s, allowed us to record music, speech, stories and random thoughts. Videotape brought life to our ability to record what we believed was important, so we could share it later. Our desire to record what is important to us and play it for our family and friends is partly how we create the common bond of shared experience. Technology expands our ability to capture and share stories, but the stories remain central to our collective existence.

We will trust a new media form, but it must be earned

We don't trust a brand until we understand it. In the 17th and 18th centuries, people had few ways to learn about a new product, no matter how germane to their lives. They were reliant on education, slow-moving word of mouth or the occasional handbill. Later we added the news business to our growing list of sources, and now it's all but impossible to ignore the most influential brand messages online. We are willing to trust new media and the messages they carry, but only if we can depend on what they tell us.

The best branding is often repetitive and becomes part of our subconscious mind

Some of the best advertising is so subtle we don't realize it is happening. Historically, when companies started to scale they realized they needed to brand their products. The earliest days involved stamping the name of a company right on the product, like Hershey's does now on its chocolate bars. The branding was direct—enjoy our chocolate and you know from whom it came. It seems so overt, but in reality we become used to that type of branding and don't consciously recognize it. Yet subconsciously, it registers, whether on a chocolate bar or on a social media site.

We will always complain that media outlets are proliferating

I doubt the inky wretches standing around the first printing presses worried too much about it, but eventually people started worrying about the proliferation of newsletters, pamphlets and newspapers. Historically in the U.S., those who had the means to start a newspaper usually did, with the combination of technology and freedom spawning new publications as the channel formed. The same happens today, in all kinds of multimedia and social media channels. Nothing has changed. We still like to complain, but we adjust to the new media environment anyway.

The ability to create wealth drives scalable innovation

When revenue opportunities increase, so does the professionalism within the industry. As New York City's advertising industry boomed, it matured under the guidance of J. Walter Thompson. The same process emerged in Philadelphia, with N.W. Ayer. Today, Marc Benioff helps the world see the value of the cloud and the improvements it can bring to sales productivity. Revenue growth drives professionalism and insures that leaders invest in education and mentor increasingly talented teams around them.

When we get too cluttered, we innovate our way out of it

Just as people act differently when they get crammed into a busy city, they adjust their behavior when they reach content overload. And eventually, they iterate and upgrade their tools and processes to cut through the clutter. Ironically, complexity and clutter often drive clarity. Remember Nike's famous "Just Do It" tagline? They adopted that slogan to cut through the clutter, a simple phrase that has survived decades of branding turbulence.

Our memories of brands and experiences are imprinted early and stay with us forever

Think of the music you love today. You probably added a few favorite bands and albums over the years, but the same tunes you liked in your youth are now part of your iTunes collection. Great brands imprint their music onto our subconscious, and we never forget them. Likewise, if brands are worth it, they are with us for life. And that heritage matters, too, because we often romanticize the memories of our past. The better the story—the better we are able to turn a brand message into something more personal—the more we unlock consumer opportunities.

> We always need controls, regulators or rules
> to keep us from going too far

It never fails. Give us enough rope and we'll hang ourselves. So, since we generally try to have too much of that good thing, a little regulation will remain a part of life. We complain about it, as we do with almost any restriction, but in the recesses of our minds we sense the wisdom of controlling our excesses. So while the unscrupulous snake-oil salesman eventually loses all trust, effective regulation can help establish it.

THE TIMELESS TRENDS IN THE MODERN AGE

The past couple decades of exploding technological advancement haven't touched the core truth held within these timeless trends. In fact, the sheer mass of information today—not to mention the speed at which that information can change—only reinforces those core truths. To be sure, though, the recent advances in technology, science and culture have radically changed the forces that buffet those timeless trends, as well as the way consumers process and react to them.

> New narratives drive
> consumers to search and
> share more and more
> diverse sets of information.

Hope and aspiration — The sheer number of people unleashed, both personally and professionally, as they go online will boost audience ambitions at an exponential rate. Just look at the scope: The number of people online topped one billion for the first time in 2005. We passed the two billion mark in 2010, and hit 4.2 billion by 2018. Approximately 200 million people join us online every year—the equivalent of adding a Brazil to the virtual world every 12 months. Yet we still have a lot of room to run; Internet penetration currently covers just 55 percent of the world's population. We will see hundreds of millions of new people join us online in the coming years, each will bring their own hopes and aspirations. The community will fuel their desires, but they also will help drive the dreams of others with whom they interact. We need to keep up on those new users and their goals, because many of them will eventually start to reshape our collective audience.

Our stories — As we get better at sharing our stories with one another, we expand the diversity and the interests of the audience. New narratives drive consumers to search and share more and more diverse sets of information. Google already processes more than 40,000 search queries per second and 1.2 trillion searches each year. On Facebook, users share more than 30 billion pieces of content each month. We're sitting around a digital campfire, but one big enough that everyone can feel the warmth.

Trust in new media forms — We spend more time on Amazon.com, Facebook, LinkedIn, Twitter, Google, iTunes and other social properties than we do on CNN, Fox News, the *Wall Street Journal*, the *New York Times* and other media properties. We're willing to place our trust in new channels, especially those in which the content lends itself to easy and digestible social sharing. News is still relevant, but we increasingly want to add our own thoughts to a story.

Imprinting brands — We don't think of "Just Do It" as much today as we did when the line was fresh and ubiquitous. Now we get the branding imprint from the Facebook logo we see 20 times a day and the Twitter bird every time we open the smart-phone app. That imprint comes in different forms now. What is the social media equivalent of imprinting Hershey's on a chocolate bar? We need to study our users, especially the Millennials who drive new usage patterns, to understand what will be important in the years to come.

Mini media outlets — We're shifting from a world where journalists and advertisers kept us informed to one in which the 1% of content creators inform us and the 9% shape the message and make it relevant to us. In a world with more than four billion people online, we now have about 400 million influencers operating their own mini media outlets.

Wealth creation — Investors pumped tens of billions into Internet companies last year, with even more going into the software industry. If you have a good idea, the money will usually find you. And as more people build wealth, they can help bring new media and industries into a more robust and mature state.

Cutting the clutter — The definition of clutter has changed on us. Those who join the billions online for the first time might embrace applications that longtime users find inefficient or maddening. Other groups find new and better ways to share content—think of Millennials and Snapchat, where more than 180 million people participate on a daily basis to share their lives. Ultimately, clutter is in the eye of the beholder, defined by the individual user and no one else.

We listen to what we remember — We're fully on board for streaming music from Spotify or iTunes, and those services have helped maintain and even expand the audience for the great bands we listened to while growing up. But it completely changes how bands, especially new emerging bands, put themselves on the radar. Burrowing out a space in the listener's subconscious is more difficult than ever.

Regulatory boundaries — Regulators, countries and companies continually reshape the environment. So while technological advances will always outpace regulation, regulation won't stand still. Eventually, we'll see the future equivalents of the Federal Communication Commission's net-neutrality decision, the European Union's decision to sue Google over privacy issues, and the debate over ICANN's global oversight of web addresses. The more innovation we experience, the more governments and regulators will try to make sense of the new legal landscape. At times, they will overreach. Other times they won't go far enough and consumers will pay for it. Either way, governmental oversight and innovation will always have a rocky relationship.

The pace of change will shape the way we interact with the world, with brands and with our online communities. Yet all these timeless trends will continue to flow under the surface, guiding human behavior through new environments shaped by new circumstances. But we have to remember that it's this malleability that makes the trends timeless. How they're borne out today is different from yesterday, and it'll be different again tomorrow. When we have 200 million people coming online each year and new channels emerging at what seems like a daily pace, our audience will constantly change. Our story has to change as well.

The Mad Men advertising era is over. The Storytizing era is here.

THE IMPORTANCE OF STORYTELLING

By Rick Kaplan, one of the top network television producers of all time.
He has collected 47 Emmy Awards working for CBS, ABC, CNN and MSNBC,
where he served as executive producer for Walter Cronkite, Peter Jennings,
Ted Koppel, Diane Sawyer, Katie Couric and Christiane Amanpour.

Don Hewitt, the legendary executive producer and creator of CBS News' iconic television magazine, "60 Minutes," always said that the secret to success was simple: "Tell me a story." It might be a report on the most obscure or arcane subject, but if you had a way of wrapping it in a great story, people would pay attention.

From the beginning of our recorded history, man has used storytelling to catch our attention and to share the events and traditions of the human experience. Study the earliest cave paintings, which chronicled great hunts by early man to obtain food for survival. They tell stories of bravery and sacrifice as tribes with little in the way of primitive weaponry attempt to conquer and kill mammoth beasts far faster and stronger than themselves. Watch the hunter in a small section of the painting, battling to the death with a bison. Observe the scavenger attempting to immobilize his larger prey while he scrambles to avoid becoming a noon meal himself. In an instant, you are drawn into what this thousands-year-old storyteller wanted you to know about his existence.

Millennia later and many worlds away, listen to an economics lecturer attempting to make the current recession interesting to his class by describing the small details, the personal dramas and the successes and failures that make his facts and figures come alive. When you hear stories of people making due with less – stories of sacrifice and generosity that describe the lives of so many of our less fortunate fellow citizens – you not only learn about and feel their pain, you are immediately involved in their lives and suddenly care about what happens to them all because of their stories.

"If history were taught in the form of stories, it would never be forgotten."
— RUDYARD KIPLING

An abandoned dog is hit by a passing car and killed. Townspeople bury the poor animal along the roadside and make a modest gravesite. Those are the bare facts. But as legendary radio announcer Paul Harvey used to say, "Here is the rest of the story..."

A dog is abandoned by his master along a desolate stretch of highway, next to the railroad tracks that handle long haul freight and passenger trains. The little fellow is noticed by some citizens from a nearby town and, feeling sorry for the poor guy, they feed him and play with him. The dog is very friendly and appreciative. But he will not get into a car and go home with any number of folks who, by now, all want to adopt him. He is steadfastly loyal and will not leave this particular spot because he knows his master will come back for him. It is obviously just a mistake. The dog is sure his master will return. Winter comes. A tent and blankets are put out for the little guy while he stands watch for his master's return. When long freight trains rumble by, the fun loving dog jumps up and down as if to welcome the engineer. And all the engineers return the welcome by blowing their whistles, which the little guy delights in. Winter turns to spring. Then, one day, horror! The dog has been hit and killed by a car. The townsfolk are distraught! They gather together to bury their little friend, and they put up a simple cross to mark the spot where he lived his last year. It's a simple story, and the heart of it lies here: People honk and think of their friend when they pass by. And every day, twice a day, those big freight trains go by and, out of respect and love, they blow their whistles to remember.

(That's a story originally reported by famed CBS News Correspondent Charles Kuralt and was part of his "On the Road" Series.)

"Stories are a communal currency of humanity."
– TAHIR SHAH, in Arabian Nights

The point I'm trying to make is simple: No matter how cutting edge a technical advance is – no matter how extraordinary one's business plan has been – it's not the ones and twos or the X's and O's that make a project soar. It's the personal stories, the human facts and experiences that ultimately attract and attach us. It is the difference between baking a cake with no frosting and no flavor, or serving up a fresh strawberry shortcake dripping with whipped cream and fruit.

You will always enjoy a good dessert!

Chapter 5

THE NEW DEFINITION OF OWNED MEDIA

"Individuals play the game, but teams beat the odds."

- SEAL Team saying

I grew up learning how to play team sports. My dad, a minor league baseball player for the Yankees and the baseball coach for our high school, taught us how important it was for every player to be ready to support the other eight on every play. What would we do if there is a fly ball? A grounder to the infield with a runner on second? A bunt or a passed ball? We drilled our responsibilities over and over, all the scenarios, until we understood our role and that of every teammate. We kept it simple, practiced it endlessly and, when the time came, ran it seamlessly.

So I was wired from my early youth to know who else can make a difference and support them on every play. But I also learned that the times you forget or ignore your role, you pay for it. In baseball, the ball sails past the cut-off man and the runner scores. In business, we complain about silos, follow trivial political agendas or fail to deliver the data our colleague needs, and it costs us sales and profits. Even small mistakes accumulate at the bottom line.

Naturally, I patterned much of my management philosophy on these baseball terms. But many years later, while preparing a client presentation about the transformation of digital media, it struck me that the same teamwork metaphor aptly explains marketing today. The way successful websites would evolve within a Storytizing environment started to remind me of our infield rotations on bunts. And in that context, I started to glimpse a powerful redefinition of owned media.

WAKING UP TO THE PRECOMMERCE DAWN

Like most models, we made the idea of owned media too complex over time, and complexity indicates an underlying laziness. Websites are a perfect example. Some three years after CERN (the European Organization for Nuclear Research) created the first site in 1992, a fledgling e-commerce site emerged. Called Amazon.com, it sparked a fascination with getting people to visit us. We even developed our own language on how to describe success or failure with websites. Is the visit direct or a referral? What's the bounce rate? What's the click-through rate? What's our cost per conversion? Before we knew it, we were walking into meetings to listen to people tell us about page views, single page view visits and page exit ratios. If you had to develop a language to confuse people, this would be it. We stopped talking about customers as people and started talking about them as inanimate objects or metrics.

> A new audience niche had started to have as much influence on our brand story as we did, and it was time to take notice.

We did this because it was easy, and in an age of booming e-commerce growth in the U.S., we could get away with it. We could create our site, wait for customers to arrive and, occasionally, tweak a few pages to attract a few more people and land that bonus. But our customers never cared about our metrics, and few companies would go the extra mile to really understand where their customers actually were.

And then the PreCommerce Era arrived. Suddenly we were forced to admit that more than 99 percent of the time customers spent online was not on our websites, even when they were considering a purchase. They found out about our brand and our products elsewhere—in places where, at the time, we could not control the message. A new audience niche had started to have as much influence on our brand story as we did, and it was time to take notice. We had to redefine our approach to marketing via digital media, and we had to redefine owned media.

THE NEW DEFINITION OF OWNED MEDIA

The website no longer resides at the core of owned media. In a Storytizing world, owned media is anywhere and everywhere the customer wants to interact with that brand. We no longer control the message, even on owned media, so we must pay even greater attention to the customer experience with our brand story and the consistency of our message across every channel on which it appears. Providing the highest degree of experience and consistency will help ensure our story is well-told wherever the customer finds it. But to reach anything close to a guarantee in this world, marketing professionals have to work seamlessly with a new set of teammates, both inside and outside the corporate walls. Here's tomorrow's lineup—which, of course, has nine players:

1. *The influencers who co-create your story.* Journalists and individuals generate articles, posts and videos that tell a version of your brand's story, but from their perspective. We can no longer lazily reach out to the 50 influencers who drive most of the conversation about our brands. We're now in the talent development business. We identify the best storytellers for our brand and strive to get them to frame the narrative. But we can't stop there, either. We have to nurture relationships with the next 50, and the next 50, to get the subsequent generations of creators to be aware of and on board with our story.

2. *The advocates who share your story.* If you're counting tweets, likes and comments to appraise how well your program worked, you're only seeing the tip of the iceberg. When we look at the 1-9-90 model, we want to go beyond the surface and identify not just the 1%, but the 9% who exert the greatest influence over brand narratives today. Who are the 1,000 or 10,000 or 100,000 advocates who will shape the content related to your brand? Are you giving them the resources they need? If they already like what you do, do you give them even more to empower them?

3. *The judges who decide if your story is worthy.* We used to think of reviews as the be-all end-all. In reality, reviews have become old school. Consumers now review brands on a real-time basis through comments, shares and likes. Marketing professionals need tools that provide a constant assessment of the community that judges their brands, so they can understand who makes the key judgments and how they've come to their conclusions. You can't shape customer experience by analyzing red/green/yellow sentiment on a PowerPoint slide. You assess how your brand is being reviewed by constantly measuring the judges, their rulings and how the audience reacts.

4. *The employees of your company.* The most underutilized teammates in the corporate world are our own employees. Companies still worry that their employees might speak out of line with the corporate message. They overlook the fact that employees are already speaking out or choosing to remain silent on key topics—and either way they've sent a message to the world. When your company faces a crisis, thousands of employees supporting the business online can tell an infinitely more powerful story than silence. We can get much more creative and successful if we empower our employees' voices in the external world.

5. *The content creators within your company.* We used to think of content creators as those who developed messaging and materials

for our website, an advertising campaign or news release. Today, we can have dozens, if not hundreds, of employees who write blog posts, create how-to videos, author white papers and produce other forms of content that impact the myriad micro-segments of our target audience. Your engineers, designers, procurement managers or IT professionals all can reach their like-minded peers better than you ever could. They have the credibility and already speak the common language of their community. It's always powerful when a non-spokesperson can speak directly.

6. *The spokespeople for your company.* Yes, they still play a critical role, too but it's no longer enough to simply be on message for the company. We need to ensure that we are telling a common story across all our properties and from all of our people. It's no longer a one-person show; your spokespeople lead an army now.

7. *All your websites worldwide.* Customers can smell a lack of alignment a mile away. When they hear a great story from one content creator and visit our site, the experience has to remain consistent. We used to fall back on the easy excuse of time and resources—it takes too long to change the content on all our sites, or we don't want to distract visitors with alternative content. Today, that's rubbish. We can see what people like, what they search and how they enter our site, and then we can provide them precisely what they prefer when they arrive. We call it "responsive experience," and it's a basic requirement across your entire online presence.

8. *All your intranet sites worldwide.* Whatever we share externally should be available in a similar manner within the company. Whatever our customers are thinking, saying and doing should be available for every employee to see. We need to end the days of people or teams hoarding information about public reaction and marketing analytics. Exposure to reality empowers your staff. Think of your employees as customers, and make their experience at least as good as your best days online.

9. *All of your shared channels worldwide.* Each channel provides a different experience. We might encourage more conversation on Facebook, share more how-to videos on YouTube and dive deeper into a topic for a guest column on a blog. But we absolutely must retain a consistent message across every one of those channels. A different forum might provide new ways to think about the topic at hand, but each angle must complement the others and your overall brand narrative.

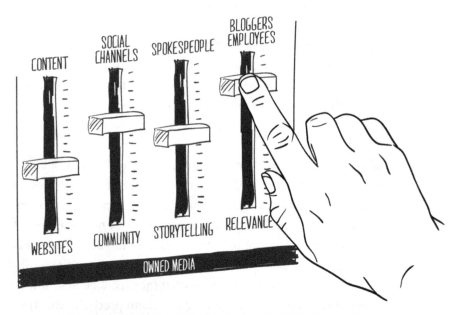

OWNED MEDIA HAS BECOME AN EXPERIENCE

Our marketing voice is now both portable and malleable, so our definition of owned media—what we control—has to change to accommodate the new Storytizing reality. We now control the official experience with our brand, but we might not even control the initial customer interaction anymore. Don Draper and his Mad Men colleagues loved controlling that first interaction with a new brand message, but that flavor of cigarette doesn't exist anymore.

So we recalibrate our goals, focusing on sharing our version of the message directly with our customers in the locations where they prefer to interact with us. We become storytellers and distributors, but we also realize we have to let go. After all, a message rippling across Facebook can reach far more customers than will ever visit our website. So we reach out to customers at every step along their PreCommerce journey—while they're learning, sharing and just having fun. If we wait until they visit our website, our ability to influence their final purchasing decision could not be worse.

In this Storytizing world, owned media is transformed from a site into an experience.

In this Storytizing world, owned media is transformed from a site into an experience. Any content we create and approve is owned media—whether in the form of a spokesperson's statement, a one paragraph post on Facebook, a group discussion on LinkedIn, or the customer's experience on our website. And like any well-functioning team, owned media needs a manager. I see a day when one person manages all owned media across websites, spokespeople, shared channels and any other location people encounter, shape and share the brand story.

But make no mistake: Ownership no longer implies full control. If a company creates content of any type, it's owned. But that will no longer keep the 9% from reinterpreting and reshaping it.

USING OWNED MEDIA EFFECTIVELY

How we effectively use owned media defines its success. Here are five key examples of how to optimize the new version of owned media.

1. *The Supply Chain of Language* — Typically, customers search the same 15 keywords or phrases to find your story or a related topic. It's more important than ever that you develop a supply chain of language, so you use the same keywords on your website, in your social channels, as tags for new content and in your press releases and statements. If you coordinate across your owned media supply

chain, you'll greatly increase your search engine optimization. Communicators are becoming the new search experts by necessity, because telling a good story doesn't mean much if an audience can't find it.

2. *Network Coordination* — Are you sharing the same messages and a similar story across your website, social channels and via your spokespeople? Are you able to provide consistent content, but customize it by channel so it matches up with your customer's PreCommerce journey? We have to expand our expertise into how customers choose to learn about our brands, and then develop the right network strategy to reach them.

3. *Understand the Role of Each Channel* — Are we teaching via YouTube, answering questions on forums, and just having fun on Facebook? What is the role of each channel? Are we imagining the customer journey, documenting what really happens online and then adjusting our message and delivery to match up with the customer's needs?

4. *Customize Customer Visits* — Customers search for certain keywords that lead them to our sites. So think of those key words as a sort of digital handshake, an initial greeting that starts to forge a bond. This little bit of information allows us to provide the exact content they want when they visit our site. Are we doing this?

5. *Focus on Customer Experience* — Are we consistently monitoring all the media we own to ensure a consistent experience and response? How do we know if we've succeeded or failed?

When I think of doing this well, I think of the advice that Gayle Fuguitt, Chief of Customer Insight & Innovation, Foursquare, offered at our PreCommerce Summit in 2015. She said, "Brands are built in the brain." Our critical first effort to help build our brands in the customer's brain depends on how seamlessly the nine players on our owned media team work together. Do they support each other, working as one to build brands in the brain? Or do we have nine players running around in an uncoordinated manner, hoping they randomly stumble into the right play?

THE OWNED MEDIA SNOWBALL

By Kurt Holstein, an industrial engineer who co-founded Rosetta Marketing in 1998 and grew it into a Top-10 U.S. digital agency before selling it to Publicis. Before Rosetta, Kurt spent 16 years at Procter & Gamble in brand management working on consumer health care brands like Crest, Scope, Pepto-Bismol and several pharmaceutical brands.

Bob raises a very important point in his discussion of the changes affecting owned media. He makes the point that we are moving well beyond the days when we had the ability to "create and control" our owned media. That way of thinking made sense when the content was *static*. When we could develop a website, a sponsored blog or a video and then send it out into the world to be visited, read or watched. After all, it was called owned media for that very reason: We created it and we controlled it, therefore we owned it.

Today that very same type of content is anything but static. *It's dynamic. It's evolutionary.* It starts to grow and evolve as soon as it's released. That same website, blog or video, when released today, immediately starts to attract comments, posts, tweets and shares. So, what we originally "owned" quickly grows into a broader collection of content that becomes the new brand experience. It's like a snowball rolled from the top of a large hill. The content we started with, which will always be at the core of what comes next, is transformed and grows into something much bigger, and different, than what we started with.

This transforms our concept of create and control. We can no longer control the message, so what's a marketer to do? For starters, we must seek to influence the experience a consumer has when they interact with the brand. We still can help shape the content as it evolves by influencing where the consumer finds the content and providing a more consistent experience across all the channels through which a consumer experiences our brand.

And we need to do that by harnessing the power of data and technology, and we do that in three core steps:

1. Starting off with more strategic and consistent initial brand content;

2. Integrating Paid, Owned and Earned into a more interactive and supportive combination;

3. Leveraging longitudinal personalization of content, at all key touchpoints, so consumers get a consistent and relevant experience wherever they touch your brand.

We can create a consistent collection of initial brand content by working with the nine players Bob has put on today's owned-media field. By providing clear and strategic messaging directly to the nine players, we can at least ensure we start with a common pool of core messaging and content.

Regardless of how solid a starting lineup we field, we have little choice but to integrate our paid, owned and earned media if we want to shape and manage dynamic content as it grows and evolves in a digital and social environment. For example, social media amplification allows a brand to turn up the volume on the content and conversations that it believes are on strategy. Amplification is nothing more than spending media dollars in support of initial brand content, or on-strategy earned content, each of which increase the reach and frequency with a targeted custom audience that's much larger than the general group of consumers already engaging with your brand. By definition, as the volume goes up for on-strategy interactions, it turns down the volume for off-strategy experiences.

Finally, longitudinal personalization can be achieved using new, more advanced content-management applications. Bound, a leading multi-channel personalization platform, enables marketers to segment online audiences and target them across most interactions via a three-step approach:

1. Website and marketing data is turned into insights that identify top-performing segments and content sequences, as well as roadblocks and untapped places to reach new customers;

2. A user-friendly business decision rules engine allows marketers to design campaigns that deliver the right content to the right person at the right time; and

3. A suite of integration tools enable cross-channel personalization by linking the decision rules with the other parts of your marketing technology stack, such as CMS solutions, web analytics, third-party data providers and more.

So, the next time you think about your owned media, think of it instead as your *initial media*, the snowball that you're about to roll down the hill, and think about how you can influence its upcoming journey as it evolves, grows and becomes the consumer experience that will ultimately shape your brand.

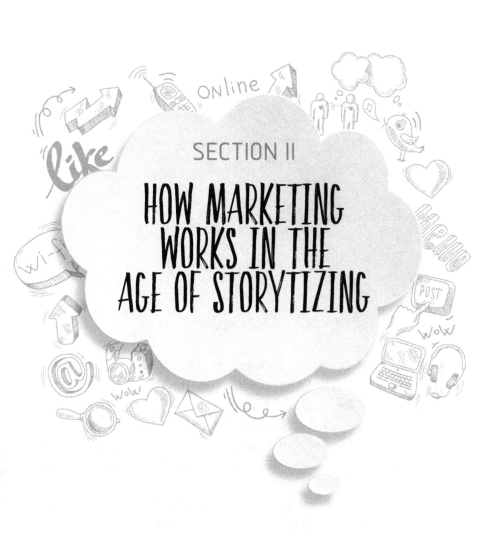

SECTION II

HOW MARKETING WORKS IN THE AGE OF STORYTIZING

Chapter 6
SNAP(CHAT), CRACKLE & POP MEDIA

*"Change before
you have to."*

- Jack Welch

Whenever I run across Kellogg's Rice Krispies, my mind immediately pictures Snap, Crackle and Pop, the cereal's cartoon mascots. They still make me chuckle, because they remind me of those carefree days as a kid, long before we worried about gluten, genetically modified organisms and sugar content. We didn't need a whole lot more than a few dancing animated characters to seal our choice of cereal.

The sheer span of their history make Snap, Crackle and Pop a premier example of branding. But those three names also hint at a deeper, more technical lesson for marketing professionals. It turns out snap, crackle and pop are also three of the six "derivatives of position" in physics. Very generally speaking, the derivatives of position help describe the ways objects or groups of objects move. The first four relate to, in order, *velocity, acceleration, jerk* (the rate of change of acceleration) and *jounce* (the rate of change of the *jerk*). For the most part, classical physicists focus only on the first three derivatives, so they gave the remaining trio a nickname—snap, crackle and pop. Because those higher-order derivatives have little use for most physics researchers, there's little consensus about them.

Market research often runs into its own snap, crackle and pop problem. We can easily identify velocity in how quickly today's technologies allow us to disseminate and access brand messages. The rapid development of new apps, devices and capabilities accelerate that already rapid pace. And brilliant scientific innovation paves the way for leapfrog technologies that prompt new "jerks" in the market.

The higher-order changes in technology and the marketplace aren't always as easy to discern. Think of Steve Jobs' uncanny ability to develop the iPhone and other products we didn't realize we wanted. Somehow, he could foresee how a combination of variables would work together. For example, Corning was ready to stop making Gorilla glass until Jobs asked them to continue. Every executive in the industry knew of Gorilla glass and capacitive touch technology, but no one figured out the power of putting the two together. Meanwhile, the music industry was in the midst of a tectonic transition, ripe for disruption and in search of ways to increase—or at least stabilize—revenue. It helped that Jobs had one of the best design teams sitting there in Cupertino, but the "snap, crackle and pop" envisioned how they could come together in a single device. And now that device, or similar devices the iPhone inspired, sit in billions of pockets and purses around the world.

In today's media world, we are surrounded by a similar set of influences that have led to disruptive innovation. I see five major drivers, but the "snap, crackle and pop" of the marketplace are bound to produce others we can't yet imagine.

1. *Video compression* — We have made tremendous progress in how we compress video, making it possible to enjoy short bursts of video on our phone with little delay. We no longer worry about pixels, bits and file sizes. We just expect visual content to work.

2. *Texting and messaging* — We send over eight trillion text messages each year, worldwide. (I don't know about you, but I'm betting once you reach one trillion per year, habits are pretty clear.) We like to speak and share our thinking quickly and succinctly.

3. *The phone as our camera and video player* — Our phones now work as well as most of the cameras we used to purchase, and we're comfortable taking video at almost any time. We're chronicling our lives whenever we want to.

4. *The importance of 4G LTE* — We can download 4- to 5-times faster than with 3G, which makes all the difference in our desire to download photos, watch movies or video chat as we move around during the day. Essentially, we can have entertainment come to us, rather than finding the right time and place for it.

5. *The integration of images* — Developers are making it easier for social channels to add tools that allow users to enhance their posts, similar to Snapchat's option to geo-filter backgrounds. Based on who you are and where you are at the moment, the content you may desire can be at your beck and call. Geo-targeting, content and our lives are finally becoming fully integrated.

FIVE DISRUPTIVE TRENDS LEADING TO A NEW SOCIAL LAYER

People around the world share trillions of messages, images and videos each year, increasingly through social media and not just via text. The emerging social context engines will know so much about us that we'll come to rely as much on their judgment as we rely on search today. This will put search engines in a squeeze, trying to remain relevant with our online social lives. If you're not the *social layer* for customers—their primary channel on which they conduct the majority of their personal and business activities, from socializing to e-commerce—you will become a secondary source.

One could imagine a case in which Google becomes something like our library, while a channel like Snapchat becomes our primary social layer with new functionality that lets us communicate easily with friends and colleagues, learn what we can buy and order items we like. In essence, it becomes our everyday platform for virtually all our needs. Google, of course, is fully capable of making this happen, as well, but no doubt some companies will underestimate the transformative power of the key market trends pushing us toward a new social layer.

New social channels will integrate what we prefer far faster

All of us can explain what Twitter, LinkedIn and Facebook do. But several Chinese platforms have already moved beyond them by seamlessly integrating a wider variety of capabilities. WeChat mixes features similar to Instagram (posting photos), Foursquare (finding people near you) and instant messaging. Youku combines shades of Netflix and YouTube. And on Sina Weibo, users can post like we do on Twitter and post like we do on Facebook. When technology removes barriers, we build what we want.

Texting will become old school as social chat takes off

Right now, we think of Millennials when we consider the Snapchat audience. In reality, Snapchat is integrating images, video, text and content into one place. More and more, users of all shapes and sizes will favor this richer way of communicating over plain text.

Three seconds will be the new norm to grab attention

We already see the "quick grab" on Facebook. If you don't get hooked in seconds, you pass on a video. We are training our brains to do what we do best: make quick decisions based on limited information. Today, first impressions register faster than ever.

Entertainment will become a 24/7 opportunity similar to music

Since we can access shows, movies and music anytime we want, entertainment companies who make all their best content available will become our go-to sources. Those who make us jump through hoops will be left behind to fend for themselves.

Snapchat will lead to snap decisions on where and how we buy

If we are comfortable with a purchase and we can snap to buy, we will. Any social channel we trust could become our new place to buy, and if it integrates enough functionality it could become the primary social and ecommerce layer for many.

THE POWER OF SNAPCHAT

To illustrate how powerful Snapchat has become—and to illustrate the potential it has to transform how we communicate, buy and sell in the future—I brainstormed some future-ready ideas with my W2O colleagues. Think of this like an open letter to Evan Spiegel, founder of

Snapchat, coming from marketers and how they would like to see the channel evolve, with a few ideas of how to make it happen:

Provide greater transparency on users of its service — Transparency allows marketers to focus their advertising and brand messaging. The data can be anonymized to respect privacy, while still achieving targeting goals. But it is critical for marketing strategy and planning; it cannot be held only by Snapchat.

- **IDEA: OPEN UP A LIMITED API, ALA FACEBOOK'S 30 DAYS OF DATA.** Brands must be able to access data to plan. Facebook has shown the way on how to protect individual privacy while still preserving the integrity of the data.

Help brands develop relationships with Snapchat Stars. We all know the power of influencers. The Stories feature on Snapchat has started to produce key influencers that could have major impacts for a brand. These stars are similar to those on YouTube, Vine, Instagram and other channels. If a cosmetics company could join forces with influencers who provide make-up tips or how-to videos for skin care, they could increase both the reach and the authenticity of their message. In turn, this supports the users who drive Snapchat traffic.

- **IDEA: CREATE A PLATFORM WHERE BRANDS AND INFLUENCERS CAN MEET.** These relationships lead to more targeted earned and paid media, something valuable and worth paying for. It helps the users gain additional influence, building loyalty to the platform and their audience. And it boosts authenticity, critical on Snapchat where audiences tend to take a much more skeptical view of advertising.

Create a "Snap to Buy" feature. We need a return on our investment. If Snapchat creates a "snap to buy" feature where users can purchase products or download important purchasing information for later use, we can better track funnel activity. This can work for a brand by partnering with emerging stars, mapping them as they discuss a topic, providing an option to buy directly within the chat, and then delivering directly to the user or to a local outlet. For consumables, this scenario could also facilitate simple couponing or co-marketing opportunities.

> New models can open up opportunities—including the chance for brands to sponsor other brands.

Develop new content partnerships between talent, media networks and brands. A traditional ad won't work in Snapchat. However, new models can open up opportunities—including the chance for brands to sponsor other brands. Snapchat's media service, called Discover, hosts branded properties for Yahoo, *People*, *Cosmopolitan*, the Food Network, *Daily Mail*, Vice, CNN and others. Build bridges between the Discover properties and other complementary brands.

- **IDEA: BLEND A TV SHOW WITH BRAND X.** Brand X works with the talent on a TV show. The talent on the show Snapchats on a key topic, which also involves Brand X products. This would generate great content, keep the topic aligned with Snapchat users' interests and integrate brands appropriately.

Innovate in geo-location. Snapchat already innovated with picture filters that are automatically uploaded from your location. Since Snapchat users already accept geo-located content, new ways to build value via location won't alienate the target audience.

- **IDEA ONE: CREATE A CONTEST BASED ON GEO-LOCATION USE.** Once a certain level of use is reached, prizes are made available. Brands could provide filters based on relevant topics, such as the Olympic Games, with backgrounds that feature local athletes. Or a razor company could sponsor the Movember fund-raiser, capitalizing on the idea that men will be shaving in the near future.

- **IDEA TWO: ALIGN SNAPCHAT CONTENT FROM BRANDS DOWN TO THE STORE LEVEL.** If the retail networks of a country are aligned to geo-location, a brand can offer unique content—including coupons and other offers—at the zip code level. Users can snap-to-buy, and the product gets delivered to your closest store.

Improve how the Stories platform is handled. On the Snapchat app, Stories are essentially paid content from brands. But those stories don't appear in-line when users interact with friends, which is what they come to Snapchat to do. It's a couple clicks off the beaten path. CNN doesn't put all its advertisements on a separate page for paid content. If brands have found success with this approach, OK, but on the whole the Stories experience does not overlap with how most people use the app.

Partner with users to create a "brand studio." A "brand studio" platform on Snapchat should contain a wide range of brand content—images, video, quotes, etc.—but it also should remain open to anyone. Encourage users to add their own ideas, make requests and participate in making each brand studio as cool as it can be. Ultimately, brands could create content directly with, and within, the Snapchat community.

As marketing professionals, we have to broaden our field of vision to see the technological, scientific and cultural changes occurring all around us— both within our customer base and beyond.

To be clear, I'm not suggesting Snapchat has missed the boat on anything. In fact, the platform already hosts some brilliant marketing programs. The Call of Duty franchise teased a new release by encouraging customers to follow the Snapchat ghost logo through its maps. Taco Bell, one of the most followed brands since April 2014, launched its Doritos Locos

Taco with a 10-second video during the MTV Movie Awards. It landed the fast-food chain 70,000 followers. And Snapchat launched filters for employee dissatisfaction in an attempt to poach new tech talent. The filters displayed for users in or around the Uber, Pinterest and Twitter headquarters—showed the platform's ability to stretch beyond marketing and into human resources.

As some of the current Snapchat programs show, and as some of the future possibilities suggest, the largely unknown snap, crackle and pop of the Storytizing world will foster transformational change in how we think of social channels, how we communicate and share content, and how we engage with our target audience. As marketing professionals, we have to broaden our field of vision to see the technological, scientific and cultural changes occurring all around us—both within our customer base and beyond.

IDENTIFYING THE RIGHT METRICS FOR YOUR BUSINESS

By Chuck Hemann, Managing Director, Analytics at W2O Group and past Global Digital Analytics Manager, Intel Corp. Chuck is one of the pioneers of social listening and analytics in industry and author of *Digital Marketing Analytics*.

One of the most common questions I receive at conferences and in meetings is: "What is the right metric for us to use in order to understand the performance of our campaign?" Whether the company is a large enterprise or a small- to medium-sized business, the answer to this question is top of mind for executives and practitioners alike. The answer I give: "It depends." Much like a Supreme Court Justice who doesn't respond to hypothetical case scenarios, it's difficult to respond to hypothetical measurement queries.

The explosion of digital and social led to a data influx unlike anything the marketing community had seen. It also led to the creation of a number of new metrics and methodologies to measure digital effectiveness. However, all the new data, methodologies and metrics don't mean that we should change the way we measure marketing. Regardless of channel, digital marketing metrics should ladder up to overall marketing objectives, which should ladder up to overall business objectives. The rest is just noise in the system – interesting, perhaps, but still noise that should largely be ignored. In most cases when I receive the question about the "right" metrics, it comes with no context about the campaign's and company's overall objectives.

So how do you take this to your VP or CMO, who's also inundated with new data sources and methodologies? Here are a few ideas that can help set you on the right path:

1. **ENGAGEMENT METRICS ARE BECOMING SECONDARY KEY PERFORMANCE INDICATORS (KPIS)** – If you are a business that doesn't sell anything to consumers online, it's often challenging to identify pure ROI from your campaigns. In those instances we've relied on engagement and media efficiency metrics to understand success. That is changing. There are a growing number of vendors, including the social platforms themselves, that offer the ability to understand attitudinal shift at a very granular level. Check those out.

2. **DON'T TRY TO DO EVERYTHING** – There are a lot of very interesting analytics innovations coming from the social platforms to help you understand success. Resist the urge to try them all, even if you have the budget to do so. Identify what's available, pick what's strategically valuable, and conduct those tests.

3. DETERMINE HOW YOU'LL OPTIMIZE SHORTLY AFTER FINALIZING THE FRAMEWORK – If you create the right sort of framework you'll have primary and secondary KPIs. Which ones will be the right ones to optimize against? You should have a plan.

4. CONNECTING DATA SOURCES – Perhaps the hardest thing to do without an internal team or a lot of resources, but the intersections between data sources is where the magic happens.

Digital measurement is becoming increasingly more complex, but if you follow the tips I've outlined above – plus the steps of identifying business objectives, then marketing objectives, and then your own digital objectives – you should find the right metrics for your business.

Chapter 7

(RE)SEARCH—CREATING OUR OWN MIRROR

> *"The aim of*
> *marketing is to*
> *understand the customer*
> *so well the product*
> *or service fits him*
> *and sells itself."*

– Peter Drucker

I always thought of search as software that brings our subconscious to the fore. We use search to ask about the topics on our mind. It can help us formulate the question we want to ask, even as it provides the answer. It's a supplement brain, working hard with our own to make a complex world simpler. Humans typically can think of only 200 to 500 questions about a brand. Our research finds that customers ask the same 77 questions over and over, depending on the issue. The majority of us search for the same 15 keywords and phrases for any topic at any point in time.

We naturally fall into these and similar habits. We follow the herd, and Google, Bing and Baidu adjust to how the herd evolves. The search engines have become so good at flexing to our needs that marketers don't see how often they lose control of the search process that once seemed fairly standard. The world of search has changed, and it has changed because we've changed—in both our daily search habits and the range of content that now matters to us. Kudos to the search engines for keeping up with four billion of us.

In fact, they've evolved even more than we realize. The CMO Council estimates that $580 billion will be spent globally on advertising in 2017, and a growing share of that will shift to digital. Despite the rise of Snapchat and other social media platforms, Google still captures a huge slice of that spend—and serves as the No. 1 guide to a lot more of it. It would behoove the marketing professional to understand how Google draws and steers our target audience. Yet the search titan has gotten so smart about how we search that it adjusts to our queries without us realizing it. In essence, it acts like its own market researcher, figuring out what customers want.

So, if we want to control our marketing research, we need to track our own audience. We need to understand how to search and research correctly. We need to do better (Re)Search. Take a hint from Google and what it does on a regular basis to get smarter. Back in 1998, it served about 10,000 search queries a day. By 2006, it was processing that many every second. And this year, estimates suggest that Google will process about 3.5 billion searches per day, the equivalent of about 40,000 per second.

Conversations, tweets and all of our personal online contributions show exactly what we think.

Meanwhile, we search for whatever we want, whenever we want it—making search, as technology futurist Ray Kurzweil predicted, an extension of our brains. As 40,000 searches peeks into the human psyche every second, no wonder Google has such a clear understanding of human behavior and tendency. And armed with that, Google changes its search algorithm more than 500 times a year. Perhaps it adjusts to accommodate more mobile sites, to better integrate Twitter or to place more emphasis on certain conversation styles. Where once Google relied heavily on links, it now has added the massive amounts of content and conversations we generate on social channels. Google didn't want to become tomorrow's library, so it rapidly adjusted to what we share publicly.

This leads to a very subtle and yet fascinating innovation in search. Links don't change much, and they don't tell us much beyond what we publish. But conversations, tweets and all of our personal online contributions show exactly what we think. Collectively, they show how our actions, comments and thoughts will likely progress. And since humans adhere to patterns, volume is the friend of the algorithm.

This all helps search engines move closer toward a potential technological singularity, a theoretical point at which machines gain intelligence. We already teach machines when we display what we like, when we care more about a topic, how we like to shop and everything else that we're willing to do online. The reach toward artificial intelligence runs on human brainpower and behavior. And given the massive volumes of data pumped into that process, we now have to think about search engines as another marketer—not one we can meet in a conference room, sure, but one that already knows what we and our audiences are thinking.

Throughout the history of marketing and communications, we never sat idle during such sweeping changes. Advertisers didn't watch television explode in the 1960s and just say: "Well, we'll just give you a lot of money and trust you do the right thing." The industry invented media planning and buying to make sense out of where to invest dollars to reach customers. We're in the same situation today, but we haven't developed a strategy as quickly as the online and social world has changed around us. Only now have we started to build a rigorous Audience Architecture and develop a robust (Re)Search model that benefits brands.

(RE)SEARCH AND THE DUAL-BRAIN SYSTEM

Audience Architecture forms a foundation for the new (Re)Search model. If you track your audience through this architecture, you can determine precisely what they care about—either independent of search or with search analytics included. The combination allows you to learn from both environments, so you can reach customers more directly and effectively through search. Think of your Audience Architecture system and search engines as your two research brains—you need both to gain a holistic understanding of your audience. The power of Google and other search engines and the insights gained from Audience Architecture already justify the dual-brain system, but there are many other reasons we're moving toward this approach:

Content and conversations will drive search results more than technical SEO solutions or links. We've made search too complicated over the years. We wonder about meta-tags and links, and we drag conversations into arcane details that bore most marketers. These are important, but we're lucky if 1% of our target audience visits our site on any given day. The other 99% of our audience is out sharing content, having conversations and searching for answers to their questions. We have to think about what we can do to impact and shape the content, the conversation and the answers to customers' questions. If we can influence those conversations and narratives, a stronger SEO position will follow.

If we want to align with our customers, we need to use their language, not ours.

Language use will become even more important as we learn to speak and share like we search. Many of us used to scoff when text messaging started to butcher our native language. Then Twitter arrived and did the same. Now, though, most of us accept the fact that a new short-form language has emerged, and it impacts how we communicate. We have no problem using phrases without verbs or adjectives. So we now have to consider what texts, tweets and search queries tell us about the language we should use on our websites, posts, blogs, news releases and similar content. If we want to align with our customers, we need to use their language, not ours. And the more we align our brand messaging with the language our customers speak, the more likely they are to find the content that is relevant to their conversations. Links used to be the key to relevance in search. Today, the key to relevance is language.

How customers access the web becomes a critical factor, so mobile becomes No. 1. Responsive experience becomes critical. Brands need to provide customers the content they want on their first attempt to access it. If we don't figure this out—if we don't create mobile apps that integrate with search—the search engines will figure it out for us. Today, almost all apps are closed systems, so we're losing the ability to integrate the best of search and the best of our own brand information into a singular mobile experience. We need apps that utilize HTML5, CSS and JavaScript in new ways to unlock this opportunity. It's starting to happen.

> Our increasing dependence
> on communication
> through social channels
> makes it even more likely
> that everything our
> audience does will impact
> our (Re)Search.

Our "hidden" conversations via text and email will start to impact search thanks to anonymized data. Providers can anonymize everything an audience says through texts and emails to protect our privacy, and then feed the identity-less data into search algorithms to improve our knowledge of what customers care about. Facebook has already done this. And as we rapidly move into new ways to interact through Snapchat, WeChat and other apps, they too could provide collective insight into what we think and how we behave. Our increasing dependence on communication through social channels makes it even more likely that everything our audience does will impact our (Re)Search.

Comparing how our audience acts outside and inside search will show a more holistic truth. Welcome back to Audience Architecture. If our audience platform can show us what our current and future customers do on a daily basis, we can do a gap analysis to see how the things they care about align with what people search for. This will help us determine how to find new customers, how to adjust our language or how to identify trends in the communities we care about. We need our own market research platform, in addition to (Re)Search, to stay on top of what is actually happening. The differences will lead to new insights and create new angles for how to use search more effectively and explain why certain queries are more popular.

Search queries and the customer journey, when analyzed together, can lead to important conclusions. Search queries can happen at any time in the customer's decision-making process. If we look at the timing and the patterns of queries and how they relate to the wants and needs of our audience, we can judge where customers are in their assessment of a brand, event or topic. Put another way, once you know the online journey of your customers, you can overlay it with actual search queries over the same timeframe and determine whether you properly participated in the process and the market more broadly. A marketer might judge correctly that future customers began an information-gathering phase in March. But if he didn't deliver the content the customers wanted—as indicated by their social media and search patterns—he lost the advantage of his initial forecast.

We will care deeply about every brand mention, anywhere it takes place, and use the knowledge gained to make decisions on earned, shared and paid resources. How many conversations about your brand start each day? How many new pieces of relevant content emerge, and which ones really matter? How and how far does that critical content spread? We have to become experts about how our brand's story is told and shared after it leaves our sphere of control. We have to measure the impact our message truly makes, where it has the most influence, and then measure the impact with greater precision. If we have two channels with equal volume, we can experiment in earned media, watch for impact, and then utilize paid media where it will have the best chance for success.

Protecting our search position by combatting the impact of negative news. Every negative comment or article decreases your value in search and in your share of conversation. What can you change? Can you help educate a person who is negative but off base? Can you place new, positive content in the market to replace the negative content over time? We need to understand what to do here, yet we tend to discount the negatives and place all our time on the positives. They both matter, and if negatives start to spike, even a relatively small amount of volume can have a significantly higher social-signal score.

BACK TO BASICS

Sometimes, we need to understand what we can do well, and what we can't do at all. In order to keep up with technological singularity, we can't try to outrace a search engine's algorithms. We can't afford doomed attempts to outguess a machine approach built by some of the world's smartest engineers and constantly refined through the processing of more than 40,000 data points a second. Rather, we build a robust Audience Architecture to complement what the search engines can't capture.

That's why we marketers steeped in digital media love the principles of judo as a metaphor for what we do. The first principle: never oppose strength with strength, for the stronger person will always win. Instead, achieve your own balance to take advantage of an opponent's weakness. Develop your own center of gravity to gain your balance. We need to track our current and future customers so we can find our message's center of gravity. We need to develop our Audience Architecture to understand our opponent's (i.e., the customer's) tendencies. And then we need to leverage our strengths and their behavioral patterns—both through (Re)Search and Audience Architecture—to deliver our brand message in the most effective manner.

The mirror that search analytics holds up to our marketing program captures just one view. To get the full view of our effectiveness, we need to look in our own mirror as well.

A 3D VIEW OF HOW INNOVATION IS EVOLVING

By Manny Kostas, former CMO of Symantec Corp., senior vice president of marketing for Hewlett-Packard Printing and Imaging, and Global Head of Platforms and Technology for H-P's print business, where he leveraged external innovation, print technology, physical sciences, solutions software and big data to identify how businesses, including 3D printing, will grow.

Bob is prescient when he asserts that "consumers are re-creating usage models, technologies and information delivery at a speed that rivals the high-tech industry. They learn how to advance their own initiatives, often subconsciously, from their peers." As marketers look to create new and compelling use cases for 3D printing, they will need to work to devise an approach where they have an ongoing dialogue with their ultimate customers, who are the designers, creators and manufacturers. Every week, new materials and formulations are being invented that will enable the creation of parts and objects in ways not envisioned today. How does the marketer create a campaign or a media plan that will satisfy those unspoken needs and applications while leading to rapid market expansion? I doubt anyone can. As an industry, we will need to engage in a dialogue with trusted peers, using their terminology in the forums they frequent, with the devices they choose and when they choose to use them. We cannot rely on what a prescriptive media plan would suggest. Agility and dialogue will rule over a deterministic brand monologue.

As these new use cases reveal themselves, we will need to execute this agile dialogue to deliver agile content via rich media types, such as YouTube. Smart friends will educate each other with how-to videos, proudly showing what they created and then breaking down the steps needed to make it a reality. These smart friends are our best salespeople and marketers. Their peers, ranging from maker-movement hobbyists to aerospace engineers, will be looking for ideas on how to create a yet-to-be designed part. All of the communications channels the inventors use will need to be just as Bob describes – agile in a way that old media could never be. The notion of the traditional marketing campaign, along with its content and delivery channels, will have to evolve to match that agility.

Peter Drucker's popular quote is applicable for search and agile content, as it is a reminder of what new, technology-driven markets such as 3D printing will face. In my estimation, adoption of 3D printing will not be stimulated by traditional mass marketing of a static value proposition. It will require agile marketing that divines yet-to-be articulated uses. The content revealing these uses will be fostered by a dialogue between those who envision a product and the technologists who can help them assemble the puzzle pieces of software, materials and printing processes. Together, they will create 3D objects that existing design and manufacturing technologies cannot create. Drucker will be proven right once again –"The aim of marketing is to understand the customer so well the product or service fits him and sells itself." Dialogue and agile content delivery will be the difference between those who capitalize on new markets like 3D printing and those who follow the leaders.

Chapter 8

WORD OF MOUTH, PREDICTIVE AND SMART MEDIA PLANNING

> *"Never make predictions, especially about the future."*
>
> **- Casey Stengel**

> *"If you don't know where you are going, you might wind up someplace else."*
>
> **- Yogi Berra**

ew companies put together any data-backed predictions prior to kicking off what they hope will become a viral campaign. Most, if not all of them, are measured only in retrospect, with little of that knowledge fed back into forecasting the next effort. This bugged our team, but probably no one more than Andy Boothe. Andy worked as a quality control software engineer at IBM before moving to the Texas Emerging Technology Fund, where he built databases to quantify the fund's performance. He left the fund to work at W2O.

Andy is a bit of a polymath. He likes puzzles. He speaks Elvish, the language spoken by the grey elves in J.R.R. Tolkien's fictional Middle Earth. He's a master dancer and karaoke singer. But more than anything, he knows how to build an algorithm. Our teams talked for months about "word of mouth" and what it means. Andy and I both agreed that what passes for a word-of-mouth campaign is, more often than not, little more than a good effort that gets lucky. We figured we could apply some science to it, predicting word-of-mouth rather than measuring it after the fact.

Around the same time, Seth Duncan, our managing director of analytics, was trying to figure out how we could more accurately predict which social and digital media channels matter throughout a movie's lifecycle. A punk rocker as a youth in Portland, Seth not surprisingly enjoys tracking entertainment media. So he'd set to work on figuring out a way to predict the channels that would buzz in the week leading up to the film's release, toward the end of its theater run and then again during its launch on DVD, Netflix or the like. He wanted to go beyond identifying the results in retrospect, so he started to think about how he could predict those patterns for movies yet to be released.

Seth, Andy and I went off and started dissecting these problems on our own. We knew they all had a common thread, but I don't think at the time we were all working on the same sticky problem.

TINDERBOX, TARGETED MARKETING AND PREDICTIVE PATTERNS

Many years ago, during my time in the pharmaceutical industry, I picked up a lot of chemistry terminology. I still use the term "chirality," one of my favorites, now and then. A molecule is chiral if another molecule is similar to it in composition, but not quite the same. Our researchers always used the example of our left and right hands. They look the same, but they're different and we use them for different things.

The notion of chirality came back to me as I pondered how we could reliably predict the flow of online marketing campaigns. I'd hit a rut while thinking about the Meme, our influencer algorithm and one of the most important products W2O has developed. We use the Meme to identify the influencers in a particular area, and then drill down by country or language. And while I thought of how we could refine it, I thought that a chiral approach might work instead. Let's take a tool similar to the Meme, but rather zeroing in on smaller segments, why not think in the opposite manner—going from town, to city, to state, up to country and even the world.

I had no idea if it could work, but Andy isn't the type of guy who comes up with reasons a thoughtful idea can't work. So he said he'd start tinkering around on Java and playing with some different iterations of a chiral counterpart to the Meme. I put it in the back of my mind and went on with my work.

> His new idea focused not on how conversations were disseminated at a large scale, but how a small audience absorbed the idea—and how they might then ignite word of mouth. He called it Tinderbox. It was a spark of genius.

A few months later, Andy called me over to show me the new concept he developed. His new idea focused not on how conversations were disseminated at a large scale, but how a small audience absorbed the idea—and how they might then ignite word of mouth. He called it Tinderbox. It was a spark of genius. I was blown away. Andy had isolated all of the towns in Texas and indexed approximately six million articles down to the town level. With that in place, we could identify the content that mattered by topic and by town. So now we could pick out the influencers for each topic at the town level, who influenced that influencer, and we could simply click on a map to find exactly what they posted about the issue—and we could refresh the data on the fly.

Andy clicked through Tinderbox to show who has influence in Odessa or Dallas and what they'd been tracking in the past days or weeks. He not only could identify the hot topics from one town to the next, he could pinpoint who shaped the online conversation and how. He'd killed two birds with one stone:

The current designated market area (DMA) approach was now old school.

Marketing professionals relied for years on the DMA model to segment opportunities for their mass-media advertising. The potential of a DMA stemmed from the population of a city or market area, using basic demographics rather than actual content consumption. With Tinderbox, we now could show the power of earned media in its rawest form. Rather than looking from the top down, we could look from the bottom up. Content consumption (interest) trumped population.

We found when earned media outlets, such as a newspaper or blog, wrote about content that the townspeople cared about, the outlets would continue to share similar content. If no one cared, it would alter its habits. This Darwinian approach, familiar to all news, seemed obvious enough, but we could see it in real time and with a more nuanced view of what worked and what didn't. If an organization was discussing "immigration reform," we could see the 22 towns where that conversation buzzed the most and pick out the top 10 to 20 influencers in each by town.

So when a major campaign for Brand X launches in the U.S., we can know, in advance, the particular set of 543 towns that are most likely to fuel future sales and word of mouth for the campaign—all based on their location and their influence on the 340 million people in the country. Once the campaign launches, we look at the content created and consumed in each of those towns and identify those that reached or exceeded a predetermined threshold important for the campaign's success, the ones that didn't care about the campaign's primary objective, as well as the rest with middling results. We know immediately how to adjust our earned and paid media to catalyze more positive behavior, adjust our campaign message to something that resonates where it previously had bombed, and reignite interest where it received a lukewarm response, all at the town and, ultimately, the store level.

AUDIENCE:
80M IN U.S.

MICROSEGMENTATION:
10 TYPES OF CUSMTOMERS

SMART FILTERS:
25K IN LA WHO LOVE PRODUCT X

AGGREGATE CUSTOMERS:
100 CITIES X 25K

2,500,000
TARGET CUSTOMERS

And we now had a real time media-planning tool to judge word of mouth and inform decisions.

Andy's work with Tinderbox gave us a powerful tool to track marketing campaigns in real time. And it could start to give us some predictive capabilities based on the more granular local data we could accrue over time. In the meantime, though, Seth was busy trying to untie a pretty complex knot. One of our clients in the film industry asked us to figure out which social channels would matter to each of its movies as its theatrical release approached, and which ones would matter later, for a franchise or releases in other formats. For movie companies, this was a marketing Holy Grail.

While Seth worked the problem, I kept thinking back to an Austin company called Qcue, led by Barry Kahn. I met Barry when I was a volunteer member of the Emerging Technology Fund, and his idea for the company caught my eye. In a nutshell, Qcue helps sports teams and ticketing firms adjust to shifting demand, changes in market conditions and other real-time sales data. The model worked well, so a few fellow advisers and I worked to get the fund to support the company.

The challenge for Seth and the team was a little more mysterious than selling excess tickets for a San Francisco Giants game, but the two shared a core philosophy—identify patterns of behavior, and then compare and contrast those patterns over time to predict likely future activity. Essentially Seth wanted to study the film-audience patterns by genre, movie, director or any other variable that might shape how consumers act and think—even before the movie's release.

On our first pass, the team went overboard. Prior to our first meeting, Andy and Seth said they'd indexed every movie that had ever been released in the U.S., on the order of 10,000 to 12,000 movies. Too much data can be as bad as too little, of course, and their massive collection kicked out a lot of noise. We did have a good laugh at this complete geek out. So Seth narrowed down the index and ran it for all the known variables that would cause a person to see a movie, buy a DVD or game, or see a sequel. He got an exceptionally strong result, and we could now see which social channels mattered for a movie along any week of its lifecycle.

With this and Tinderbox, we'd learned more about what predictive analysis is really about—predictable patterns. We can't predict the future, but we know human beings follow certain sets of patterns. What we like, we'll do over and over again. A Batman fan will probably see all the Batman movies, and they'll tend to like other superhero franchises as well. Now, we can identify the critical 1% and 9% in these various subgenres and gauge early indicators of changes in interest. Put another way, we can build an Audience Architecture to follow all fans of a movie franchise, so we can learn from them on a daily basis forever after.

HISTORY IS THE BEST PREDICTOR OF THE FUTURE

Anticipatory metrics of what we'll do next are only as good as the historical index on which they're based. Google anticipates what we'll want next because we *already told them everything* through our search behavior. We can get smarter every day by identifying our fans, indexing them in a custom search engine and letting them tell us what they want, which characters matter the most, what they think of a new game and how they are learning about a new movie. It's the biggest focus group ever created.

The combination of Tinderbox and our Predictive Movie Model made it clear that leveraging earned, shared and owned media can make paid media smart, but not the other way around. When you can see what people read, watch, talk about and share—and follow that audience by channel and on a micro-segment level by channel—you reap precise data you can match up with your paid media plan. W2O already has started employing an ESO-P gap analysis, which helps show where we can use paid media most effectively. I believe this will go mainstream, and media planning will evolve from PESO to ESOP.

KNOWING THE CARD COUNT FOR YOUR BRAND

By Seth Duncan, a data scientist who trained and worked at the University of Pittsburgh Medical Center and the University of California at San Francisco in data science and statistics, respectively. He is now Chief Analytics Officer for W2O Group.

And by Andy Boothe, leader of R&D and head of data science for W2O Group. Formerly worked as a software performance analyst at IBM and as investment manager for the State of Texas' Emerging Technology Fund. Andy is also fluent in Elvish.

Being great at predictive analytics is more like being an expert card player than being a Nostradamus. It's impossible to use mathematical models to prophesize "the next big thing," whether it's the next most valuable company, an Arab Spring, the emergence of a sharing economy or even a Sharknado. Rather, statistical predictions work best under a relatively narrow set of conditions, including fixed systems of variables that interact with each under repetitive circumstances. So it does well in the natural sciences, in medicine, card games and, under the right circumstances, in marketing.

Predictive modeling can guide us as we try to ascertain which strategies will perform well in the near-term – if you have a long history of similar events to start from. Estimates of how many clicks you'll get for a digital ad placement or who will donate to a cause after an e-mail marketing campaign are good candidates for this sort of math. In each case, analysts can look at hundreds or thousands of previous similar events - what you would call trials in scientific experiments, or hands in a game of cards - and make a reasonable prediction about the outcome based on what we know about current conditions.

The competitive advantage of predictive analytics for marketing is a lot like counting cards in Blackjack and shifting your betting strategy on the composition of the remaining cards in the deck. For example, the number of people who viewed a digital trailer in the week leading up to the release of a certain type of movie might have shown a high correlation with ticket sales. If it did, you might allocate more of your future media budgets for similar films to YouTube. Just like in card playing, shifting the odds in your favor will not win you every hand. But, as long as the rules stay the same and you stick to the same strategy, you ultimately will beat the house.

It is this ability of predictive models to use the past to predict the future that makes the rise of social media so important for marketing analytics. In the past, data had to be painstakingly collected at small scale and great expense to build marketing models. Today's large-scale adoption of social media means that such data now spontaneously appears in tremendous quantities, essentially for free. This has reduced the cost of model building dramatically, allowing marketers to stack the odds ever more in their favor.

However, no amount of data or modeling is a substitute for a crystal ball. Using models to predict "the next big thing" will always be a fool's errand. Humans are always innovating, which changes the rules of the game. A small change like a new latte flavor at Starbucks won't affect models much, but truly large inventions like Facebook and Netflix restructure the rules in ways that make your historical analyses irrelevant. How much you weigh wouldn't be relevant anymore if gravity disappeared.

In the short term, companies who get smart about modeling have much to gain, but in time these skills will become table stakes. Companies that invest in learning both the limitations of prediction and how to act on new predictions quickly and decisively – and recognizing when the rules have changed forever – will make the smartest bets.

Chapter 9

AGILE CONTENT IN THE NEW MEDIA WORLD

"Change your thoughts and you change your world."

- Norman Vincent Peale

ost innovation is incremental, not sexy or dramatic, but each forward step can create unique advantages for a company and open new opportunities. In today's high-tech world, these incremental innovations occur at lightning speed, and sometimes we fall into a false sense of security as we hold onto tiring models that don't quite work as well today as they did yesterday.

A Bain & Co. report called *Trillion-Dollar Growth Trends to 2020* estimated that $5 trillion of incremental GDP generated in the current decade will stem from a premise of "everything the same, but nicer." Sure enough, we often scoff at that sort of iteration, discounting it as something less than true innovation, yet those small steps accumulate into remarkable journeys. Linus Torvalds, a Finnish-American engineer and hacker developed the Linux Kernel in 1991, leading to the most widely used open-source operating system in the world. Andy Rubin and his colleagues founded Android, Inc. in 2003 to utilize Linux-based software for touchscreen phones and tablets. Now part of Google, Android is the most widely used mobile-phone operating system in the world.

We don't have a hard time keeping abreast of all these innovations, mostly because they're developed by public companies with outsized personalities—but also because we often use the service or software ourselves. We don't do as good a job at understanding how these innovations have changed our habits, and those of the average consumer. And this is far more profound, because consumers innovate, too. They don't do us the favor of organizing into public companies and trumpeting everything they do each day, so their innovation often goes overlooked or is poorly understood. Yet consumers are re-creating usage models, technologies and information delivery at a speed that rivals the high-tech industry. They learn how to advance their own initiatives, often subconsciously, from their peers.

A great example is Megan Parken, who runs Meganheartsmakeup, a YouTube channel she started to provide beauty tips and life skills to her friends. Megan started her channel from her home in Austin just three years after Google bought YouTube in 2006. She was 13 years old at the time, and now at 22 she leads a channel that has nearly 800,000 subscribers and her videos have more than 120 million views. She has also been a columnist for *Seventeen* magazine.

Megan's massive audience rivals the reach of many of the top print magazines today. *Fortune* has approximately 857,000 subscribers. *Food and Wine* magazine has almost 950,000 subscribers. But Megan can provide videos daily whenever she'd like, not just weekly or monthly. Plus, her audience is highly responsive to what she sends out, since they can share her videos, comment on them and take them in a new direction.

Megan said she started her channel because "video for me was something I felt comfortable with. I also felt there was a connection I made with the viewers that was very important to me. People often comment that they see me as a 'friend' or a 'big sister' and that means a lot to me," she explained.

Megan is just one example of how media outlets can form around highly specialized and personalized approaches. They're often centered on the talents of an individual, more than a staff. Thousands of them have formed on YouTube, Pinterest and other channels, and most have loyal, responsive audiences ready to hear about what's relevant to their needs. Their subject matters might vary. The size of their audience certainly does.

But they all share a common attribute: They're agile in a way that old media could never be, and they're more agile now than even digital media was five years ago. Our marketing campaigns have to match that agility.

RESPONSIVE MARKETING PLATFORMS

Chicago native Tim Bahr has been a pioneer in creating visual stories for companies since the mid-1980s. His first company, Orbis Media, partnered with the *Journal of the American Medical Association* (JAMA) to provide the week's top health news to television stations throughout the U.S. and beyond. (These were the days of video news releases and background footage, where television producers accepted pre-packaged news and then edited it to their liking.)

Tim eventually went on to create another company, MultiVu, owned by PRNewswire, which elevated the concept of giving reporters worldwide access to a rich set of content on a given story. But his next company, NextWorks, flips the whole concept on its head. He and his colleagues created a platform that can deliver a full story for a topic, issue or a brand directly to the consumer in their channel of choice. Their "content capsules" can be embedded in any social channel, website, intranet or email. Most important, they can track what people think of the content via their actions. NextWorks measures time on site, preferred content and what users share. And, if they choose, they can change the content dynamically, based on what they learn.

This approach signals a new era of responsive marketing platforms that adjust to the habits of an audience. Currently, NextWorks makes those adjustments manually, but with the development of the right algorithms they and other firms will be able to tweak their content and campaigns automatically and in real time. We and our marketing platforms will judge when different content is required—for example, when a paid ad could work—all based on current consumer behavior. Companies could identify rising interest in a Facebook promotion, realize they're not converting enough to sales, and then provide special deals to up their conversion rate. The deal lasts only as long as necessary, and then automatically ends.

Advertising will shift to this new form of Storytizing, where we provide earned content in shared and owned platforms, and then adjust to what our audience tells us in return.

A brand already can share its full story directly with customers. It soon can add, on a widespread basis, an impactful and interactive experience to sell a product via Facebook or the myriad other digital channels. Advertising will shift to this new form of Storytizing, where we provide earned content in shared and owned platforms, and then adjust to what our audience tells us in return. We can already see signs of this transformation into a mainstream audience, for example:

- People are spending more time on capsules than they ever would anywhere else. A range of five to seven minutes is typical.

- It costs far less to reach the audience we spent millions of dollars to reach in the past.

- Brand teams are getting smarter by watching and learning what matters to their audience, making their next steps easier to figure out.

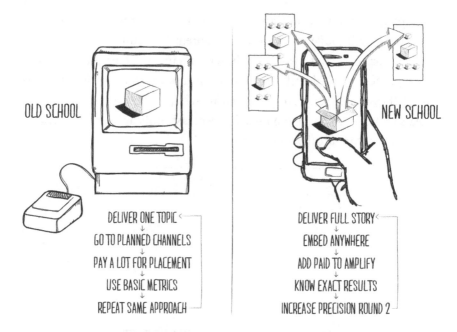

OLD SCHOOL

DELIVER ONE TOPIC
↓
GO TO PLANNED CHANNELS
↓
PAY A LOT FOR PLACEMENT
↓
USE BASIC METRICS
↓
REPEAT SAME APPROACH

NEW SCHOOL

DELIVER FULL STORY
↓
EMBED ANYWHERE
↓
ADD PAID TO AMPLIFY
↓
KNOW EXACT RESULTS
↓
INCREASE PRECISION ROUND 2

THE INCREMENTAL INNOVATIONS THAT ARE CHANGING TODAY'S MEDIA WORLD

Its 9 a.m., so the W2O team in our Austin office grabs their second (or third!) cup of coffee and heads into the Moontower conference room. They've come to learn how an interactive panel of Millennials interacts with our client's technology. Based on what they see, the team will quickly work with our creative team to build agile content, which we can drive into the conversation less than four hours after our team spots a trend.

The team learns that, if you can see a trend emerging and you can provide relevant content in a short-time frame, the audience responds positively, shares the new content and expands the content elasticity of the conversation. The 1% and 9% want relevant content to continue and enhance their conversations, so brands have to watch audiences efficiently, create relevant content and then get out of the way. These "micro trends" go away as fast as they emerge, so proper timing is critical.

If you look, it's not hard to notice how agile content has multiple definitions and how the world of media, as we have known it, is changing right before our eyes. It's incremental innovation, but these five ongoing shifts will only accelerate in the next few years.

The definition of a media outlet will change

If we define our media outlets by the people they can reach, how often they reach them and whether that audience is relevant to our brand, then we have to start including emerging non-journalists, like Megan Parken, among those who influence our target audience. And we have to go beyond typical audience numbers to judge their effectiveness.

A new media ranking will develop

Once we drop the pretense that an outlet must meet certain standards to join our rankings or media-planning activities, we'll start looking at metrics such as reach and accessibility. So we will need a new ranking system, one that's not driven by paid media but answers a new set of questions:

- Can we contribute earned media to this outlet?

- Can we share key content from this outlet on our owned and shared properties?

- Can we recommend other influencers to participate in this outlet?

- What is the "sharability" of content on this site by topic and sub-topic?

- What other outlets also routinely benefit from content sharing?

- What is the cost of a paid advertisement?

- What is the type of advertising we can do?

In a Storytizing world, marketers will have to assess a media outlet's agility, its total reach and its ability to align with their audiences. They will develop new algorithms that show the real impact of each media outlet, in terms of how it reaches our audience. They'll stop counting clicks, visits and views, realizing those measures represent a fraction of what will move sales in the future.

The full story for a brand can be shared anywhere, anytime, in any channel

You will serve the story to the consumer, rather than asking them to come to us. Every click or move you ask a consumer to make will lead to lower rates of use, time or conversion. Providing the full brand story directly to a customer creates a responsive experience for them, but it also provides feedback you can use. With emerging audience analytics tools, you won't have to guess what content the audience finds relevant; you learn directly from the customers who benefit.

Campaigns will become continual, not episodic

A campaign that takes six months to prepare and approve will miss the market by the time it comes out. It might include some awesome creative content and wake up the market, but it won't be fully aligned to capture and capitalize on the audience response. Now that we can precisely track audiences and let them inform us, we can rely on a tested library of content and respond within four minutes, not four hours. Even on longer campaigns, which remain highly valuable, we'll know how to track our audience and make our content relatable down to the minute, which optimizes our spend. It's not either/or—agile campaign models are the friends of large scale campaign models. Catalyze the market, deliver the story, embrace the trend.

Advertising spend will serve a more surgical role as a catalyst

Since we can see what the audience cares about and provide them with relevant content, we can juice successful instances with paid advertising. We won't throw money at something that's not resonating. Media planning must become agile to align with how paid, earned, shared and owned media can now work together.

THE ERA OF AGILE CONTENT

Just as the kernel Linus Torvalds created morphed step-by-step into the world's largest mobile operating system, incremental innovation is reshaping the marketing profession in a Storytizing world. Only now the Torvalds are the analysts who build new interactive panels that deliver unique insights into an audience; the fearless media entrepreneurs like Megan Parken, who see a better way to reach an audience; and the seasoned veterans like Tim Bahr, who understand that a slight change in your approach can produce a major shift in how we reach consumers.

The incremental innovations in the marketing industry will only accelerate in the years to come. As marketers, we would be wise to heed Pablo Picasso, who said: "I am always doing that which I cannot do, in order that I may learn how to do it." Test fast, fail fast and learn fast. And hey, if we're going fast, it wouldn't hurt to take a little advice from Mario Andretti, too: "If things seem under control, you are just not going fast enough." Those who remain comfortable doing what they already know what to do, watching other companies race past them, will find they are no longer in the race at all.

In a Storytizing age that demands agile content, they'll be left in the dust.

Chapter 10

WHAT MILLENNIALS ARE TEACHING US

"Play is the highest form of research."

- Albert Einstein

I n 2014 and 2015, I had the privilege of serving as a volunteer teacher for "Marketing College", a one-week course held at the U.S. State Department. Kip Knight, president of H&R Block, and Ed Tazzia, chairman of the P&G global alumni network, invite a bunch of us in to work with spokespeople, researchers and other State Department experts. We discuss the fundamentals of positioning, marketing and protecting a brand—only in this case, the brand happens to be the United States of America.

At the 2015 seminar, Nancy Zwiers led a fascinating discussion about how children learn. Nancy knows more about how we learn in our early years than all of the parents I know combined. She worked for years at Mattel, the No. 1 toy company in the world, leading worldwide marketing for the Barbie doll brand. She re-launched Polly Pocket and helped establish the top-ranked Cabbage Patch brand as well. Clearly, she possessed a keen understanding of childhood learning and behavior patterns, and to help explain them she'd developed a theory called Play Value. Play Value combined the discipline of evolutionary psychology and child development with empirical data gathered from toy sales. Nancy, who also invents toys herself, used big data before we'd ever heard the term. You can do that when you sell 120 million Barbie dolls each year.

What Nancy shared really resonated with me, partly because I had also just joined up with my 22-year-old daughter, Brittany, to start a blog series called Millennials Unplugged. In each blog post, we take a topic (e.g. entertainment) or a channel (e.g. Snapchat) and discuss it from dual perspectives of the Millennial and the Baby Boomer. The exercise helps both of us see past our normal obstacles and learn about the other generation; and hopefully it allows readers to do the same.

Play is nature's way to ensure we learn what we need to learn to survive. . . It helps us survive, and it's fueled by curiosity and the satisfaction and thrill we find in discovery.

So while Nancy talked about childhood learning patterns, and I filtered that through my blog conversations with Brittany, I had an epiphany: Millennials learn in much the same ways my generation did. From infancy, we're hardwired to learn how to play and explore. Play is a biological drive, Nancy said, coming from the inside out. Entertainment, on the other hand, moves outside in, because we receive content, process it and decide what to make of it. Both processes have immense value for youth, but they're different.

"Play is nature's way to ensure we learn what we need to learn to survive," Nancy explained. The original play patterns, she said, are rooted in exploration and discovery. It begins upon birth. It helps us survive, and it's fueled by curiosity and the satisfaction and thrill we find in discovery.

When Nancy put it in those terms, it destroyed some of my generational assumptions. We all learned in remarkable similar ways, even if the source of our entertainment has changed along the way.

Baby Boomers like me watched cartoons on Saturday morning, choosing from one of three channels. I loved Speed Racer and Jonny Quest; if I missed them in the morning, I had no on-demand options. But hey, we didn't know better. We went outside, made up our own games with the neighborhood kids and the same learning process continued.

Millennials grew up with a much broader set of high-tech options, as almost any parent with younger kids today can tell you. They could choose digital or physical play, but either way could immerse themselves within the game, whether online or in the backyard. My daughter and her peers expected to be able to customize almost any play situation. Brittany's childhood play environment was radically different from mine, but our learning instincts were essentially the same.

PLAY AS FUTURE-MARKET RESEARCH

When young kids watch a movie, they yearn for an inspirational lead character to whom they can relate. Imitation play is a critical learning tool as we develop. So while the movie "Frozen" was mostly about Anna's story, the merchandise centered on Elsa, the more relatable and inspiring character. During the imaginative play years, around three to six years old, kids often gravitate toward attributes of speed, strength or skill, or toward characters who nurture and support others who are vulnerable.

As Nancy noted in her conversation, Princess Diana offered up the perfect example of what kids seek—and why so many loved her from afar. Her status as a real, beautiful, modern-day princess helped, of course, but so did her flaws. Having a weakness allows us to love other characters more, Nancy explained. Superman is a fine character; his weakness in the presence of Kryptonite makes him more compelling.

When we think of the next generation of customers and business leaders, our thinking too quickly defaults to their expectations for personalized and customized experiences. We know they will want a technologically augmented experience and will pass on anything short of that. And so, we dream up ways to put more microchips in more gadgets and merge the Internet of Things with their world of play. We immediately think of all the entertainment options. And indeed, their expectations for play, exploration and discovery will lead to far wider acceptance of technology than with any previous generation.

More and more in the future, brands will have to accommodate new uses of technology in their messaging. Millennials provide us with some invaluable research about the usage patterns that will become mainstream in the future. We simply have to gain a better understanding of how entertainment and media sources are changing, as I discuss below. But as you read this, keep in mind that learning patterns remain remarkably similar from one generation to the next. We have to think about the inside-out as much as the outside-in.

Advertising–
Ads will become highly interactive and more personal

We can already see the rise of the six-second ad. Ads scroll as you move onscreen. You can learn whether a brand you like and want to purchase is available nearby and at what price. It will become normal for ads to interact with us, teach us what to do and show us where to go to complete a purchase. The days of advertising to simply generate awareness are ending.

Media Planning–
The user experience will drive the device or channel we target with our ads

Media planning will study what customers do online, in close to real-time, and serve up the appropriate interactive experiences on any device or through any medium that provides content. The best marketing pros will identify and understand audience behavior clearly enough to integrate a brand story into the user experience without it coming across as just more promotional chatter. Millennials won't care if these interactions occur while they are watching Netflix from their phones, streaming satellite radio or Snapchatting with friends, as long as it is relevant and not disruptive.

E-Commerce–
The ability to buy will match our timing and desire to buy.

Buy buttons will become a part of every social channel we use. Customers will expect to interact with a brand on their schedule, so following multiple clicks to find an online point of sale becomes prehistoric. They will decide to buy when they feel like it, and do it with relative ease, whether via a social channel, app, search result or messaging service. Their social layer becomes the next "retail frontier."

Content–
We will learn how to present data
that fits the situation and the device

Completion rates for vertical video ads run about 9 times higher than horizontal ads. Our content—whether earned, shared, owned or paid— must fit the nuanced usage patterns of the devices customers prefer to use. We have worried for too long where an ad will show up on a website or search page. Now, it's not just where the ad shows up, but how. A horizontal ad signals a company trapped in old school thinking. It's a small detail, and one that's easy to fix, but left unchecked these sorts of oversights can antiquate your brand image.

Communications–
Messaging apps will become more powerful than email

Messaging apps always made the crowd more informed and, hopefully, a little smarter, but Millennials have put that process into overdrive. Email doesn't allow the sorts of crowdsourcing that can give us greater insights. Messaging apps lead to conversations that don't clog up an inbox. As Millennials are already figuring out, both personally and professionally, we can use improved messaging apps not just to share relevant content faster, but to narrow the group of recipients to those participating in the conversation. Throw your pre-formatted distribution lists away. We'll work in a world where we may have 10 messaging apps, all integrated, that keep us in the loop with the right teams. Millennials will lead us there.

Problem Solving–
Collaboration will improve as we use live streaming,
game-type formats and better visuals to solve problems.

A pilot can sit in an office in Nevada and command a drone in Afghanistan. We can play World of Warcraft or Call of Duty with friends anywhere in the world. The ability to visualize data, "gamify" it and make it relevant to business will lead to new ways of solving the most intractable business problems. We will achieve as a worldwide team what we can't achieve solely via software. Software as a Service (SaaS) will never be able to do what humans can do in partnership with it.

Curation–
Brands that can curate value from user-generated
content will become more effective in the market.

Snapchat brilliantly curates the best of its user-generated content and then shares it so other users can get updates on a city or event. Brand managers used to accumulate all that knowledge themselves and use it to create their own ideas and campaigns. Now, they can identify important emerging content, curate it and skillfully share it with the audience in real time. It's faster, and it tends to embody a greater authenticity than 99% of the content companies produce. I don't know what the job title will end up being, but we will soon see "Content Curator" on job posting sites.

The New Brain–
The Internet of Things is accepted, in advance,
as a way to reach technological singularity.

Millennials want to get smarter, and they are comfortable letting sensors and algorithms monitor what they do to help them gain knowledge and create a better experience. As long as they get smarter and their experience improves, few of them will take time to care that a brand unobtrusively integrated its message into the interaction. We can put in any sensors, use beacons or other mechanisms to track behavior if we provide more value in return, not just to sell more directly. This is a very important and thin line. Marketers who don't get that point will get slammed and shut down.

THE DIFFERENCES BETWEEN MILLENNIALS AND BOOMERS

By Brittany Pearson, a 22-year-old Millennial who studied communications at Texas Christian University and is now an Analyst at W2O Group. Along with other Millennials and her father (and author of this book) Bob Pearson, Brittany contributes to a W2O Group blog series titled: "Millennials Unplugged."

My Dad and I were talking about social media and realizing how different our perspectives could be about the same exact thing. I guess that's not all that surprising for a daughter and a parent to differ on a topic, but my dad suggested we start a new blog series to reflect on how technology is changing our world and what it really means to Millennials and those who have "more wisdom." (My dad's words; I would say those who "are older.") Here are some examples, using the simple idea of watching a movie, that show how we can think similarly and yet act differently:

BIG SCREENS STILL WIN – We did a survey and found that 63% of Millennials said their favorite place to watch a movie is on their TV at home, while 25% would rather visit a movie theatre. When we're going to sit down for 90 minutes and watch something, the couch and a big screen will always be more fun. Sometimes things don't change even with technology.

WHO KNOWS WHAT WE MAY BE THINKING ABOUT, THOUGH – We are always on a second or third device while watching the TV. Most Millennials in our surveys are on Instagram or Twitter, checking up on their latest posts. The rest are split between Snapchat, texting and even shopping online. Basically, no matter what is on the big screen, something is competing for our attention on the small screen.

BECAUSE BEING IN THE MOMENT MATTERS – A positive way to think about attention spans is that Millennials like to be in the moment. Snapchat caters to this need by revealing content quickly. Boomers post on Facebook days after the event occurred and that seems to be OK, but Millennials prefer "snapping" over texting, since most believe their snaps go away and their snap "stories" won't be seen by elder generations.

PLUS WE HAVE MORE "FRIENDS" TO KEEP UP WITH – In today's Facebook world, many Millennials have between 500 and 2,000 friends. This happens because "who you're friends with" becomes the open door to becoming a friend. This reliance on "mutual friends" as a qualifier is leading to much larger friend groups. Mutual friends can be classmates, teams, companies and other groups. The good news, from the Baby Boomer's perspective, is that Millennials do seem to want to know their friends; they don't just let anyone in and they rarely meet someone for the first time via Facebook.

WE ARE CREATING OUR OWN LANGUAGE – It's time to embrace the new dialect. The auto-correction technology in phones is making it easy to develop common slang on how to communicate more effectively. Just like Google knows what we are typing in when we search, the same is true for phones, increasingly. Boomers would be wise to understand this language with the same intensity that companies want to understand the words driving search, since the language of text and the language of search are becoming one.

Like most things in life, we just have to listen more closely to each other, and it's not all that hard to figure things out.

Chapter 11

THE POWER OF LOCATION

*"The two
most important
requirements for major
success are: first, being in the
right place at the right time,
and second, doing
something about it."*

- Ray Kroc

I met Andrew Thompson at the Phoenix Conference, a meeting in Arizona that focused on medical device innovation. He approached me out of the blue and said, "I'm thinking we should work together." It didn't take me long to see he was an exceptionally brilliant entrepreneur, and soon enough his firm, Proteus Digital Health, had become a W2O client.

Proteus makes an ingestible sensor that, upon reaching the stomach, is activated by digestive fluids and starts sending a unique signal. Through a patch the patient wears, the sensor can send health information through by smart phone, monitoring body position, activity rates and other physiological metrics. It can even help people track whether their loved ones took their medicine 2,000 miles away. By capitalizing on location-based insights and data, Thompson completely changed how I think about all kinds of remote sensors, lenses and the Internet of Things. And it made me re-think my concept of location.

I always visualized location in mostly static terms. Even when something was on the move, it was always where it was. But listening to Thompson got me thinking about location in relative terms—not just a single position in the world, but how that spot influences the way our minds and bodies work, as well as how we interact with the surrounding environment.

> Real innovation changes
> how we work, play and live.

Proteus made me think of location in relative terms, considering not only a single position but how that spot or that person interacts with its surroundings. It might manifest itself through an elevated heart rate or through the pulse of our neighborhood. We can learn about our bodies, connect with people in new ways and build different relationships with brands. Real innovation changes how we work, play and live, and I needed a more dynamic conceptualization of location to follow along.

LOCATION, LOCATION, LOCATION

Whether we like to admit it or not, many of us contribute to the immensity of today's direct marketing world. The industry Aaron Montgomery Ward essentially started in 1872 with his Montgomery Ward catalog has exploded. We'll collectively spend $2.8 billion on email marketing in the U.S. alone in 2017, but our batting average hasn't gotten any better than Ward's was in the 19th century. In 2013, for example, companies sent out 838 billion marketing emails. Of the B2B emails in that bunch, which in theory can be better targeted, firms generated a click-through rate of just 1.7%. That's 98.3% of recipients who do not click-through. On a global basis, across all advertising formats and placements, the click through rate is 0.06%—less than one click per 1,000 impressions. The click-through rate for a promoted post on Facebook is 0.79%. A full banner ad is 0.04%. Yet we keep doing it because it's so cheap; the ROI is there.

So we've come to rely on a model that doesn't really care whether millions of customers despise direct marketing, so long as *just enough* of them click to make it worthwhile for the company. The financial return became more important than the return on customer appreciation. But in the Storytizing era, consumers will have tools to shut us out if we don't align with their interests. At some point, marketing professionals will need to calculate not only the returns from direct marketing, but the unseen losses from customers who shut off our valve.

Location-based insights will lead to a more relevant, location-based marketing, which will replace direct marketing as the preeminent way to reach people. We will exit the era of "dumb location marketing," and leave behind all the direct mail, robo calls and spam, spam, spam. Dynamic location-based marketing will require intelligent listening, often powered by location-centered technology, such as the Proteus sensors. We will come to understand our customers better than ever, even while we relinquish more control of our message to them. These location-centered technologies will reshape our marketing world in myriad ways. Here are but a few examples:

What we used to find out inside the doctor's office will now be delivered to us anywhere.

It's fun to check how many steps we walked in a day, but that doesn't truly transform our health. To do that, we need our entire body's set of signals interpreted and triaged, so we can access the same data and advice that we traditionally got in the doctor's office. The spreading adoption of more wearable technologies, made increasingly popular by our fascination with an Internet of Things, will help us build our personal digital health centers. If we want to know our heart rate, blood pressure, body-fat percentage, hydration levels, exercise patterns, pharmacokinetics of our drugs and so much more, we'll only need to pull out our smart phone or laptop. Innovators will start building a system of apps designed to help monitor and manage specific disorders or health outcomes. And ultimately, as we're starting to see from initial programs at the new University of Texas Dell Medical School in Austin, the healthcare delivery system will start to shape itself to this new patient-empowered reality.

We will create precise lens networks that let us listen to highly specific audiences.

It's cool to say that we know what is happening on a certain street in a certain town, but it doesn't tell us much beyond its own context. But with new lens technologies from SnapTrends, Geofeedia and other firms, we can narrow our digital data-gathering specifically on the 3,500 U.S. movie theatres that feature a particular new film. We can gather instant audience reaction from what the audience says on Twitter, Facebook, Instagram and other public social channels, and we can filter that from comments made by people nowhere near the cinema on opening night. Similar lenses could focus on consumers shopping at 11,000 Walmart stores worldwide, or in any combination of voting districts around the country. We now have the ability to fine-tune our digital media observation to almost any audience.

The concept of a neighborhood is being redefined.

We can see who influences people at a neighborhood level, but location is dynamic. A person's "neighborhood" can change, depending on where they are and what they're doing. Our set of influencers will change as we leave the beach, go home and change, and then head to Dodgers Stadium for the baseball game. And even when we're stationary, different sets of friends will influence us depending on the topic at hand. Marketing professionals can analyze the dynamic spheres of influence to find patterns of use and behavior.

Halos will allow consumers to align with and take control of the brands they prefer.

New technologies will soon allow customers to create virtual halos that follow their phones. Within the halo, a user will be able to decide what information, friends or brands to let in, depending on circumstances and location. When consumers control the experience, they will readily block coupon pollution and determine whether they will inform others of their location.

What we learn inside and outside the store
will make us more fully informed.

Marketers will begin to gather and study insights gleaned from how customer behavior changes inside and outside a story. A customer's use of apps, coupons and social media often changes as they enter or exit a brick-and-mortar outlet. Comparing and contrasting those patterns can deliver a fuller picture of what motivates a person to visit a store, buy a product, attend an event or do nothing at all. The ability to read both "on" and "off" activity will lead to a new generation of metrics and key performance indicators.

Indoor positioning systems will
improve our in store experience

Apple's iBeacon, for example, uses radio waves to track us as we walk through a store. This allows marketers to make their messaging spot-on and offer suggestions that are truly real-time relevant, not an aisle too late. That, of course, could help spur more in-store sales.

TRADING A BIT OF INTRUSION FOR A LOT OF VALUE

Most consumers will tacitly agree to this higher level of tracking because it delivers greater benefits. Traveling directions become increasingly accurate because maps can pinpoint precisely where we are. Coupons know where we are. Our apps tailor our information to our location. Our world is starting to pivot to our geographic needs with relative ease. And any time we make a technology more valuable to their lives, most consumers are happy to participate.

So, as these technologies become increasingly powerful and precise, marketing professionals will have new ways to identify their customers' dynamic location, determine when and how it's best to communicate with them, and then employ crowd-sourcing techniques to learn more about the current individual or group in play. And we'll know the exact patterns of behavior for weeks, months or years—a research history invaluable to understanding how we align with our customers now, in real-time across the coming moments, and off into the future.

But as communicators and marketers, it is imperative that we use these insights to improve the customer experience. If we don't, customers will rebel. But if we do, we will revolutionize Audience Architecture. We will talk in terms of thousands of neighborhoods, hundreds of micro-segments—and how they all align with our changing brand message.

NECESSITY IS THE MOTHER OF INVENTION ... AND GEO-LOCATION

By Eric Klasson, a veteran CEO who has worked for PWC, Pepsi, ConAgra and as a CEO in the energy industry. He is the co-founder, president and CEO of SnapTrends, and is chairman of AV Accelerator in Austin, Texas.

During times of crisis, visualizing social media content on a map can prove to be critical in saving lives. Seconds really matter and knowledge of location can make or break a situation.

The Federal Emergency Management Agency (FEMA) and other first responder organizations monitor areas during and after natural disasters, such as floods, tornadoes, hurricanes, fires and earthquakes. Target areas are isolated on social-media monitoring digital maps in order to gather actionable insights in real time. When a natural disaster occurs, the social media map lights up in the locations being affected, giving headquarters and field personnel awareness into events unfolding on the ground. Based on the information coming in via social media channels, FEMA and local public safety teams determine which resources are needed and are able to deploy them immediately.

But what if the power is out and the phones are down?

Our firm was formed to solve the problem officials experienced when monitoring crisis zones after a power outage occurred and the stakes are as high as they can get. During natural disasters, local 911 centers become overwhelmed, causing people in the impact area to turn to their cell phones and social media to call out for help. In 2011, our co-founder Brandon Burris developed a software system that geo-fenced any natural disaster impact area and allowed first responders to send text or voice messages to persons in harm's way. We received a big test later that year, when Texas first responders used our system during the Bastrop and Steiner Ranch wildfires in Central Texas (34,068 acres burned).

Snaptrends was created when Burris asked the question: "Can I create a software system that geo-fences social media content?" Three years later, it was the leading location-based social media monitoring system used by corporations, universities, non-profits and state and local governments to generate actionable insights from social media relevant to their core business.

So how does a global brand selling multiple products in dozens of countries create value for social media monitoring? In truth, the opportunities are nearly endless:

- **IN-STORE EXPERIENCE:** Listening to the customer experience in-store and in real-time is critical today. Insights during new product roll-outs or through the holiday shopping season can make or break the largest brands.

- **LIVE EVENTS:** Whether it's during major events sponsored by a brand or during the annual shareholder meeting, understanding the unfiltered, real-time customer or stakeholder point of view is critical.

- **VOICE OF THE EMPLOYEE:** Monitoring company facilities can help leaders understand employee sentiment and thoughts around their company and its activities. The Chief People Officer is best able to maintain organizational health with unfiltered employee insights.

- **CORPORATE GOVERNANCE:** Monitoring corporate R&D facilities, manufacturing plants, distributors or retail assets for loss control is essential to maintaining healthy operating margins in today's competitive world.

Location-based technologies are quickly evolving today to expand the impact they can provide for organizations worldwide. Today, progressive companies and organizations that are focused on location-based insights use this technology to gather information about product sentiment, customer experience and brand consumption. Now, organizations can capture compelling moments in real-time and discover patterns over extended time. The days of the CMO monitoring global brand mentions and sentiment are long gone. Today, every C-level executive must leverage the unfiltered insights playing out daily in social media to effectively create value for their organization at the neighborhood and store level.

Chapter 12

WHAT IT MEANS TO BE SECURE

"173 days is the average number of days from infiltration to discovery"

– Michael Crosno, **President and CEO at Kofile, Inc.**

I t was a beautiful Saturday morning in Austin, SXSW 2015 was in full swing and our guests were getting ready for W2O's first annual Geek Fest. We couldn't have picked a better day to geek-out: on Pi Day, March 14, and hitting the fateful 9:26:53 a.m. mark within our first hour. Anytime you can celebrate 3.141592653—the first 10 digits of pi—during a meeting, your inner geek has to crack a smile. We all got a kick out of it.

Those smiles disappeared pretty quickly when our cybersecurity geeks took the stage. Starting off with sobering points about the sad state of digital security today, Michael Crosno and T.K. Keanini, Distinguished Engineer at Cisco, snapped us back to reality. Michael looked out at the audience on the 55th floor of The Austonian, overlooking the Austin skyline, and gave us an overview of the bad news. On average, it takes 173 days to discover a typical hack, and another 32 to resolve it and lock down security—almost 30 weeks. So a typical hack could be messing with your corporate IT systems for more than two full quarters before it's eradicated. Businesses can fail in less time than that.

Bad actors don't just find occasional holes in our security. They come to work every day, just like us, planning out their strategy, maybe having staff meetings and exploring how to make their lives better by making our lives miserable. And they come back every day to continue their efforts. We actually battle a counter-workforce that created itself.

As I listened to Michael and T.K. plot out the potential horror stories, I started to wonder what security actually means? If there really is an entire industry focused on how to steal information at scale—and they enjoy a decent success rate—can we establish anything even approaching real security? If so, they said at Geek Fest, it will take the collective effort of an entire industry. It's no longer the domain of our IT geeks alone. We're all in this together.

IT WILL GET WORSE BEFORE IT GETS BETTER

We have plenty of reasons to be nervous. The typical enterprise computing network connects with 5.2 devices per knowledge worker, Michael told the crowd. Developers good and bad create about 383,000 new malware variants each day. And almost two thirds of U.S. companies receive 10,000 or more alerts each month. But only 8% of incidents are identified by the endpoint, firewall and network solutions deployed today.

It's definitely bad, but it undoubtedly will get worse. Basic economics tells us this: Worldwide spending to prevent or stop threats soared to roughly $91 billion in 2018, but the bad actors made at least $300 billion. If the marketplace productivity and reward tilts that far toward the wrong thing, crime does pay, and a lot. The drug trafficking market generates about $600 billion a year. Security breaches cost us more than $1 trillion annually. Cybersecurity is a real market, whether you have good or bad intentions.

The technological evidence also suggests worse scenarios to come. Barriers to hacking have dropped lower than ever. China is home to 400,000 registered hackers who are unionized, get health insurance and have access to the latest tools. If you decide to hack, you no longer have to know how to code, and you don't hide out in your parents' basement. You can find plenty of support and camaraderie.

Hackers have also developed more efficient ways to monetize the information they receive. Since they can access our databases for long periods of time, their monetization strategies don't look all that different from the ways the hacked company would monetize its assets. For example, when a breach compromises medical information, hackers can sell details of a person's health insurance coverage, and someone else can get surgery performed under your identity. The level of professionalism will almost certainly improve going forward.

Fortunately, we can evolve as the threats do. Not long ago, all of our efforts focused on threat prevention and detection. Now, company leaders have learned to deploy broader strategies to protect their company and brands—both technological and behavioral. They won't stop hacks, but a few positive trends should help marketers, communicators and executives fare a little better against the threat.

SECURING THE SUPPLY CHAIN IS A MAJOR STEP TOWARD LEVELING THE FIELD

I spent a rainy October day in Oslo with Magnar Løken, an inventor and founder of Kezzler AS. The subject of our discussion—counterfeiting and the threats to global supply chains—matched the overcast skies. But Magnar's insights and his personal story were illuminating. He's an inventor at heart. Growing up on a farm in northwest Norway, he often came up with inventions while working the land on his tractor. He got a mechanical engineering degree and eventually moved through jobs in the oil industry and for the Norwegian Patent Examiner's office.

A faulty bolt spurred him to launch Kezzler. Magnar had read a report about an airplane crash, which investigators blamed on a bolt that apparently failed. That got him thinking about how a company could serialize individual parts, have a system to trace each one of them, and then make it all impermeable to anyone who shouldn't have access. So he picked up a book on applied cryptography, quit his job at the patent examiner's office and started Kezzler. And in the time since, Magnar and his colleagues have developed a novel approach to serialization and databases that allows them to track and protect products at the unit level rather than the warehouse level. Clients use it to secure global supply chains and protect products from counterfeiters.

> Most of today's randomized code isn't really random at all— a smart hacker can identify patterns and crack them.

A simple stroke of genius made it work. Most of today's randomized code isn't really random at all—a smart hacker can identify patterns and crack them. Most of these intricate codes are generated by relational databases. But because it's a calculator process, the data or numbers are stored in these databases, and thus can be hacked. So Magnar did away with anything that could be calculated—leaving behind an algorithm that only activates with the right encrypted technology. So the Kezzler systems can produce a secure and unique code for every unit a company has in its supply chain, into the trillions of pieces.

"A database will tell you to walk into a parking garage, and then walk up each floor until you find your car," Magnar told me. "Now, we can tell you your car is on the sixth floor, row six, space five." So a manager can immediately find out where any piece or product is, and quickly pull together all the other information related to that item—including a tracking memory of what units are accessed by a user device, what was requested and where the request originated.

We will need this level of security and oversight in the near future. Pharmaceutical companies can now track and trace their products to decrease counterfeiting. Consumer packaged goods companies can learn about where their product is within the supply chain at any time. Companies of all types can now track their product units and not worry about storing the data in a relational database that could be hacked—an increasingly important safeguard as the Internet of Things unleashes a wave of networked devices, each of them vulnerable to attack.

BRING YOUR OWN DEVICE TO WORK IS LIKELY A BIG MISTAKE

Some 78% of IT professionals in one survey believed their own employees are their greatest security risk, said Michael Crosno, the Click Security CEO. Yet at the same time, the "bring your own device to work" trend has gone mainstream. That is a lot of increased risk, particularly in a world where more than half the content consumed goes through mobile devices. Experts expect that to grow as high as 80% in the next three to five years.

Andrew Hoog, the co-founder and CEO of NowSecure, a top mobile security company, builds systems for companies and governments. As one of the country's leading computer scientists and analysts, he also serves as an expert federal court witness in digital forensics, assists in national security matters and criminal investigations. He knows a thing or two about mobile security and the risks inherent in how we operate today.

Andrew and his colleagues ran an analysis in 2014-2015 that found a significant security risk in more than 600 million Samsung mobile devices, including the Galaxy S6 smart phones. The flaw in pre-installed keyboards, long since resolved now, could allow an attacker to gain access to sensors and resources on the phones, including GPS, cameras and microphones. They could tamper with existing apps or secretly install new malicious ones without the user knowing. They could even eavesdrop on incoming and outgoing messages, voice calls and data. And they could do all of this from anywhere in the world.

This example is not specific to Samsung. It can occur with any mobile software for any phone. If our computers can be hacked at this level, why not any computing device that we use? We can avoid some of the risk by avoiding unsecured Wi-Fi networks, of course, but few employees do that reliably enough. Instead, we have to rethink the entire "bring your own device to work" concept. The suggestion runs counter to current trends, including many of the trends we hope to capitalize on as marketing professionals, but when the average hack costs a large company almost $9 million it's a critical cost savings we can't overlook.

Hackers love inserting themselves into the cracks of such fragmented markets. The lack of standards and the explosion of sexy apps we put on our devices gets them one step closer to our valuable information.

FRAGMENTATION IS THE FRIEND OF THE HACKER

If the Internet of Things has us building apps for every new sensor, gadget or appliance, we exponentially multiply our security risks. We already have hundreds of companies building apps that will sit on our work-related computers and phones. Mixing work and play on our devices only boosts the potential for breaches. Meanwhile, software developers keep pumping out new apps without any real clarity on security standards.

That lack of standards will come back to bite us. Corporate technology managers need to construct an entirely new process of vetting what we put on devices that touch the company network. Hackers love inserting themselves into the cracks of such fragmented markets. The lack of standards and the explosion of sexy apps we put on our devices gets them one step closer to our valuable information.

SECURING OUR BRAND'S IDENTITY IS AS IMPORTANT AS SECURING OUR PERSONAL IDENTITY

We tend to think of security issues in terms of the intrusions that get inside our walls. In reality, spammers and others who wish to divert us to counterfeit products and scams have figured out a way to hijack something nearly as sensitive as our data—our brand's identity. They use it without our knowledge and use it to take advantage of unknowing consumers. If someone steals our personal identity information, we get angry and will do everything in our power to stop the theft. Yet, we don't get this worked up when someone steals our brand identity and uses it in a similar manner.

Hackers today will lock up sub-domains on social media sites, snapping up addresses like YouTube.com/CompanyX to take advantage of that brand. The do it across hundreds of sites in virtually every digital-media channel so they drive traffic to their sites to sell them fake products. They will create sham invoices that look like vendors' but route the money to their own accounts. They hack into your corporate credit cards and use them or sell the info on the black market.

We can protect our brands by locking up all of the domains (websites) and sub-domains (our sites on social media channels) for each country and for all the brands and campaigns in which we invest significant capital. And we can educate our employees on how they decrease their risk, so their behavior doesn't increase the odds of our information being accessed and compromised. We can still take concrete steps to reliably improve security in the workplace. Here are a few:

1. *Separate business and personal* — Don't send business information to your home. It's too easy to steal from your mailbox.

2. *Share any phishing emails with IT early* — Alert IT early to benefit the entire company.

3. *Report theft* — If your personal cell phone is stolen and you use it for work, tell IT.

4. *If a password is not required, be careful* — If you are accessing public Wi-Fi without use of a password and user ID, assume your information will be accessed and compromised.

5. *Improve your passwords* — Use passwords that are hard to figure out.

6. *Don't download torrent files* — They're filled with malware and viruses.

7. *Recycle and restore devices* — If you used a personal device for work, don't sell it or throw it out. Make sure any data on it is destroyed.

VISUALIZE OUR ANTAGONIST'S GAME PLAN AND DEVELOP OUR OWN

If we had to prepare for a war, we would no doubt sketch out detailed plans and contingencies. When we launch a new product, we rely on the research and insight to know exactly how to win against our competitors. Whether we call them competitors or enemies, we need to take an equally rigorous approach to proactively protecting our business intelligence.

That preparation should not start at our doorstep, as it usually does. We wouldn't prepare to fight after an enemy enters our village. Real preparation starts yesterday, analyzing the patterns occurring worldwide and understanding how to wage the right battles against an army of hackers who arrive at work each day to steal our information, make money and create jobs for the dark side.

Fortunately, we can develop strategic insights by sharing information on bad actors and then developing collective and business-specific plans of action. Our ability to ingest all of the data that security companies currently track, to access it via new APIs and then to figure out what it means will lead to new security breakthroughs. We can make it a fair fight. As T.K. Keanini said at our Geek Fest, "Defenders need to find hundreds of vulnerabilities and fix them all, while the attackers only need to find one. Attackers need a complete series of operations without being detected, while the defenders only need to detect them in one."

There's still hope. Our job now is to change how the game is played. Make it harder to access our information via phones. Protect our products and our brand identity. Ramp up how we detect, deflect and dismiss invaders who want our business intelligence. Think of it like any intense marketplace situation: We won't win the battle overnight, but we're going to make a little more progress every day.

Chapter 13
THE DRIVERS OF SOCIAL COMMERCE

"Face reality as it is, not as it was or as you wish it to be."

– Jack Welch

The world will change whether we want it to or not. The question, then, is whether we will embrace the revolution in marketing and use it to our advantage—perhaps even guiding the change at times—or will we make the leap to the new only when we have no other choice. For some brands, old-school approaches to branding might work better a bit longer. But even they need to recognize when the time to evolve has arrived.

More forward-looking brands have to push harder, of course. Even when we take Jack Welch's advice and face reality as it is, we tend to see the world in today's terms. We rarely push ourselves enough to truly look around the corner and open our minds to how reality will change before our very eyes. We know technology advances unlock certain innate desires. We know people respond better to a sensory experience. We know customers will snap up bargains when they align with their needs. But do we look for and find the levers that will transform the way people buy online? Do we understand what will lead to future economic gain for both sellers and buyers?

I'm fortunate enough to get a lot of time to ponder those emerging and future levers of change. Some appear more imminent than others, but on the whole I see six key trends poised to change the buyer-seller relationship.

Autonomous cars will lead to local distribution of goods and change how people shop

We know Amazon.com and other stores will send us much of what we want, but most people still get in their cars to get groceries, pick up the dry cleaning, buy stamps and conduct other mundane, but important, tasks. Autonomous cars eventually will deliver all these items to our door, which could start to radically change how stores view themselves. Does a store just sell groceries, or does it become your neighborhood valet? Could our car take us to work and then run a few errands while we're at the office?

Small businesses can sell even more worldwide

The ability to run your own business over your phone changed in 2009, when Jim McKelvey and Jack Dorsey created Square and turned mobile phones into electronic cash registers that could accept credit card payments. Removing this barrier makes it possible for anyone to sell goods or services, potentially anywhere in the world. When Jack Ma decided to allow Alibaba to start importing U.S. goods into China, he opened the door for any small business to enter without depending on Walmart or another global retailer. Assuming it is economical enough to ship, the product need only gain enough attention on Alibaba's sites, another global social-commerce platform or even a strong local platform. A Chinese e-commerce property has opened up real opportunities for small businesses around the world, proving again that we've moved into a truly global marketplace.

Smart phones, databases and our desires as consumers
will become aligned once beacons, NFC and databases
talk to each other in a manner that consumers appreciate

Near-field communication (NFC) makes it possible for customers to check out with a simple tap of their mobile phones on a payment pad or kiosk. The phones are simply tied to a credit card through Google, Apple or other "mobile wallets." As long as you have your phone, you can pay. Beacons work similarly, but with a little more push from the company. As a customer peruses a store, wireless transmitters can connect with a welcoming smart phone to receive product information and promotions. It's still crude today, but in the future smart databases interacting with these technologies will unobtrusively ask or gauge what customers want or need and can respond in kind. It will know a person's buying history, preferences and interests, greatly improving accuracy of our insights into the customer journey. When we are walking through a store, online offers should match up with our in-store shopping behavior. Simple and powerful.

Through augmented reality, the in-store experience
will refer to your virtual experience

New virtual or augmented reality technologies will give customers an in-store experience, the ability to interact with experts, ask questions and complete their shopping journey, all through a headset we buy, rent or borrow.

The social stream of consciousness will
become the next checkout counter

Chirpify is a great example of a socially streamlined multi-channel e-commerce platform that allows you to make transactions on social networks in-stream without interrupting the standard social media experience. You can make a purchase via a simple keyword or #hashtag, without leaving the site or pulling out a credit card. To take it a potential step further, impulse buying will also change with wider adoption of Spectacles or similar wearables—when we spot something we like while walking down the street, we can research it and buy it on the spot.

We will become our own manufacturers

With 3D printing we can come up with our own ideas, manufacture them, see if they sell and, if so, perhaps start our own businesses. In retail, stores might spot a trend emerging and start to manufacture a new product on their own—whether as their own line or as a stopgap while the usual suppliers catch up. The usual cue to wait for new products has been disrupted forever.

SOCIAL CHANNELS AS THE CENTER OF E-COMMERCE

Those trends promise immense change, and they're only a small slice of what's possible—most of which we have yet to know. Communicators and marketers will learn more from our customers in the next three to four years than we did in the last three to four decades, assuming we listen and interact with the right people. Our customers will teach and tell us about the trends with the most resonance, what they really want from an in-store experience, where and how they would prefer to buy during their social experience and the ideas they have for what comes next.

> If we know what our audience is doing and where—and we become proficient at sharing the right story with them at the right time—buyers and sellers will both benefit.

And amidst all that feedback, the social channels will emerge as *the* center for payment systems and e-commerce. After all, we trust the brands and properties with which we spend the most time. As more and more customers regularly interact with Google, Facebook, LinkedIn, Twitter, Instagram, Snap Chat, Apple and Amazon.com, they will join our list of most-trusted sites for commerce. Already today but increasingly in the future, customers won't hesitate to make a buying decision within their virtual walls and then make a purchase through a social channel tied to a credit card.

The next generation of retail will arise around a core social-media component, which will integrate seamlessly with stores and payment. In essence, retail will finally enter the PreCommerce world, placing the transaction in the same channels where customers reside and research brands and products. When you think about it, it's a natural alignment—but brands haltingly accept it because it's a radical departure from the status quo. Ultimately, though, if we know what our audience is doing and where—and we become proficient at sharing the right story with them at the right time—buyers and sellers will both benefit. If we pretend this isn't happening, we'll just get dragged along until we give in.

THE FOUR PILLARS OF E-COMMERCE STRATEGY

By Natalie Malaszenko, senior vice president of Digital Business at Office Depot. Natalie led Hewlett Packard's first ever fully centralized Global Digital Organization when she was vice president of Global Digital Marketing. Previously worked as vice president of marketing for Omni Hotels.

The evolution of how, when, why and where people shop online is simply fascinating. It has become a part of our everyday lives. At the touch of our fingers, we can order almost anything, anytime, anywhere, and we'll have our purchase in hand within days, sometimes hours. However, even at the rate in which e-commerce evolves today, these four consistent pillars should serve as anchors to every solid e-commerce strategy:

1. **KEEP IT SIMPLE** – The experience for a consumer today, whether desktop or mobile, must be simple and quick enough that a consumer can arrive at their destination in fewer than five clicks, and preferably with just one. Keep the organization of your site simple, direct and minimal. No need to oversell with more – in most cases, less is more.

2. **NEVER UNDER-ESTIMATE THE POWER OF INFLUENCE** – Word of mouth goes a long way. People simply trust the opinions of other people. Integrate commentary from other shoppers into the experience and provide it in a helpful way. On the flip side, make sure it's easy to leave feedback on a product or your company.

3. **CONTENT IS KING** – Compelling copy is no longer enough. Images, product videos, product 360s, and videos of the product in context of where and how it's used are now critical aids in closing online sales. Good, unique and relevant content also improves rankings across search engines. Content is definitely one investment worth growing significantly year-over-year. Plan to create, repurpose and aggregate original and third-party content to give your product more weight.

4. **EXCEED EXPECTATIONS:** This is the hardest of the four because consumer expectations have never been higher. Look for moments to surprise and delight customers, so you're one step ahead of what they hope for their retail and product experience. This is truly what sets great companies apart and creates loyalists in a fiercely competitive marketplace.

Chapter 14
HOW TO TRACK ANTAGONISTS

"You can't solve a problem on the same level that it was created. You have to rise above it to the next level."

- Albert Einstein

I sat in the classroom at the George P. Schultz Foreign Affairs Training Center in Arlington, Va., listening to my fellow instructors at the Marketing College. The "students" were an amalgam of men and women who represent the U.S. at our embassies, consulates and other facilities around the world, including hotspots such as Sudan and Pakistan. I'd prepared a course on crisis management, which naturally struck up an active conversation amongst the audience of Foreign Service workers. We discussed everything from human rights to combatting ISIL through new online techniques.

Seeing and hearing how our countries emissaries deal with some of the country's toughest international challenges gave me a new framework for thinking about today's threats to our companies, governments and other organizations. We tend to prepare for problems in a manner similar to our preparations for opportunities. We create key messages and our story, prepare questions and answers, update our websites and produce events to share our story. More often than not, we take a similar approach to negative issues, and it really doesn't work all that well anymore. I'm not sure it ever did.

Sometimes, I wonder whether companies take these threats seriously enough. People with intentions to surprise or harm our brands are actually attacking us, not just selling their own message. We can't consider them in the same mindset we do our competitors. First, we can't overcome them with a better-crafted, positive message. And second, they're usually much more difficult to identify at all, especially as the networking and obscurity made possible by digital media can make pinpointing them next to impossible. We often can't figure them out in time to fully protect ourselves.

Even the baddest of the bad—terrorists and hostile governments—market their ideas, and to do so they often use the same communication and marketing approaches we do. But the skills they employ to attack someone differ from the skills we use as communicators and marketers. They use a different playbook. For example, their advantage often rests in their secrecy, or at least a lack of transparency, so it's not in their advantage to speak a lot, move a lot or communicate in normal patterns.

Companies, including marketing departments, will have to start learning how their true enemies think and act (and by enemies, I don't mean legitimate competitors). For example, they might deploy sleepers—individuals who live in a country for years, but don't do anything to draw attention until the day they are activated. We have to think more about these and other types of potential attacks, how to stop them, how to mitigate the damage and how to respond.

KNOW YOUR ENEMY

The most dangerous attackers aren't the known high-level operatives who provide resources, encouragement or coordination to the rank-and-file. They are the rank-and-file, laying low to avoid detection, changing roles and direction with little warning and few indicators. The bosses or commanders pop up to claim credit on behalf of the group, and they become primary targets. But among the malevolent actors, they're not the ones who actually inflict the damage. They're primary targets, and deserve to be, but aren't the on-the-ground actors we have to stop to prevent mayhem.

(Let me pause to make one thing clear: I am not implying that every antagonist group is a terrorist organization. But when it comes to antagonists who seek to surprise or damage a company, they often share similar *modus operandi*.)

We need to redefine how we track, identify and analyze the behavior of these threats. Essentially, we need to become experts in anticipatory behavior.

In today's world, any antagonist group has a wide range of options to obscure their actions and intentions. Their marketers, publicists and recruiters use the open web to recruit new members of the group, catalyze media attention for a cause or even flag other members on vital issues. But they can also use the dark web to do the same thing, out of the public eye and often off our radar. They can make and use false online identities. Their operations people use the dark web to send illegal information, black market money and arrange confidential transactions. The list goes on. It's easier than ever to hide, grab the spotlight and hide again.

So we need to redefine how we track, identify and analyze the behavior of these threats. Essentially, we need to become experts in anticipatory behavior. This, combined with the proper use of analytics, can track down just about anyone online, even when they dive into the dark web. We can look at language, images, followers on social media channels and patterns of behavior in ways that help us to map out what our antagonists are doing, how they are likely to act and how we prepare for them.

This has resulted in a new model that we call Inception, based on the blockbuster movie starring Leonardo DiCaprio. In it, DiCaprio and his colleagues entered people's dreams with the intention of planting a seed of an idea in their psyche. Similarly, we want to get in the minds of our antagonists in the same way they get in our minds, in the minds of potential recruits and in the minds of the public at large.

BUILDING A THINKING MIND WITHIN OUR ORGANIZATIONS

Jonas Salk, the inventor of the polio vaccine, once said: "Intuition will tell the thinking mind where to look next." We have to build a "thinking mind" for our organization to help us prepare in a very different manner. Here's a basic blueprint for how we're doing that.

Understand and categorize the actual threats to your organization

Think of this as a 90-9-1 model, the opposite of our forward-leaning 1-9-90 framework. Generally, we know about 90% of potential negative issues in advance. We don't often suffer major surprises. A manufacturing plant explosion or random attack can occur, of course, but those events are rare.

In this flipped model, the 9 refers to the areas where the majority of organizational threats originate:

1. Trademark and intellectual property disputes

2. Litigation for a wide range of topics

3. Product issues, ranging from pricing to damaged product to alleged false claims

4. Environmental concerns related to how the company operates

5. Offensive promotion

6. Shareholder unrest

7. Employee issues

8. Rumors

9. Negative experience with the company, e.g. computer hacks or bad service

To address the 9, an organization typically creates its own radar screen, mapping out all known or potential issues that could occur and categorizes each. We can add a tenth for any miscellaneous issues, such as personal attacks and general disruptions.

The 1 is significantly more difficult. At this step, we need to isolate the "one" group for each priority issue, so we know where to focus our time and resources. We have to look at all groups potentially associated with the issue at hand, and ultimately drill down to the one. The process begins with a category analysis of all social media and mainstream media channels to understand which groups, teams of people and individuals care about the topic and might attack the organization to make their case. Upon completing this analysis, you likely can identify three basic types of advocacy against you:

1. *Groups dedicated to the cause* — In this case, a group means a professional organization that raises money, pays salaries and/or is a generally known entity with mainstream media. Once you know that the interests of such a group conflict with yours, you analyze how important it is to them. For example, the fictional "Palm Brigade" might care about the use of palm oil, but based on their public actions online you might realize it's just one of 25 priorities and low on their action list.

2. *Informal teams aligned for a cause* — This could either be a growing issue that has not yet attracted the attention of a professional group, or a chronic issue that's important to pockets of people. Either way, the concerned antagonists tend to approach these in a more haphazard way. For example, many cities may have groups

who care deeply about electronic equipment waste, but it's not clear they work with anyone beyond their local community despite having common cause with similar groups across the country. But what if those local efforts coalesce into a larger effort? Is this an issue that, like kindling wood, builds to a larger blaze?

3. *Individuals who care deeply about a cause* — Someone is offended by your advertising or had a bad experience with your product or one of your employees. In today's connected social-media world, they have a public platform to air their grievances. Companies need to identify patterns, discern whether the complaint is associated with informal groups and whether it has the potential to grow. Class action lawsuits, for example, often start small and then pick up steam over time.

DEPLOYING THE AUDIENCE ARCHITECTURE COUNTERMEASURES

The 90-9-1 model helps assess the groups and individuals that threaten a company, allowing us to rate different antagonists across a continuum of concern. At one end, we find people who are merely frustrated. They might have legitimate concerns and accept appropriate concessions and negotiation. At the other end are those who want to destroy a company for their own purposes or whims. Identifying the nature of the threat in this way can start to reveal proper strategies for confronting—or, at times, ignoring—our antagonists. Taking a hammer to a group that shares frustrations rather than a full-blown malevolence only creates higher levels of hostility, intransigence and, ultimately, threat.

With this analysis in place, we can now deploy Audience Architecture to compile critical intelligence. For example, imagine that an emerging antagonist claims it has three million supporters worldwide and can activate many more when needed. That sounds like a lot, but why take their word for it? With the use of media algorithms, we can see exactly who has publicly identified themselves in any social channel, anywhere in the world, as a supporter of the group. And we can do the same to see who has shared information in public channels in support of the group. Since this information is public and free for anyone to see, we can corral a group of, say, 5,000 public members and one million supporters and run them through a custom search engine. We might realize they have many supporters, but only a small number are active and lead on any issue.

Audience Architecture
provides us a tool to
further index the full
cohort, so we know what
issues they care about.

Audience Architecture provides us a tool to further index the full cohort, so we know what issues they care about. We can then build a market-based taxonomy that automatically filters whatever someone in the group says in relation to each topic, identify their location and rank their influence among the group. We might now find that only 400 of the 5,000 core supporters really care about the same issue we care about, and only 50,000 of the one million supporters care about the topic.

We can take it even further, identifying how those specific niches think and act online. Who do the members of the group respect, follow and share? Who are the top 50 influencers within the group for any key topic, and how do they rank in importance? How do they communicate, when, from where and through what channels? What are the exact keywords and phrases they use that impact search and help people find their story? Which people team up and why? Are new voices emerging?

THREATS OBVIOUS AND NOT SO OBVIOUS

Audience Architecture can identify and track all known plaintiff lawyers who have pursued litigation in your organization's area of expertise. Since it normally takes somewhere between 30 and 60 similar cases to build enough momentum for a class action suit, they have to publicly troll for individuals and other law firms to join them. According to the

American Association for Justice (formerly the American Trial Lawyer's Association), there are about 56,000 plaintiff's lawyers and legal professionals. This is a relatively small group to identify, track and analyze online. Why not track every plaintiff lawyer and their firm's sites to understand exactly what they do?

Given the advances of modern technology, though, an individual or small group can easily operate off the radar or use sophisticated masking techniques to pose as a more covert threat. They can work behind the scenes to get the ball rolling, connect sympathizers, spread messages and even coordinate attacks. Companies and organizations need to maintain constant vigilance and have dedicated professionals who can rapidly identify and respond to these threats as well. Yet Audience Architecture and thoughtful analysis can help identify potential covert threats as well.

Silence develops new meaning

Depending on the historical patterns of activity and silence on a particular issue, companies might determine whether a gap in conversation is typical or portends something else—a group preparing a marketplace surprise, or one whose influence is waning.

The real leaders

You can identify a thought leader on a particular topic, but you can also see who tends to start new media efforts. They might not be the same people, and an analysis of their separate and shared activity might hint at events to come.

The real issue network

As you identify cells that work together, you can start to map out a global grid that shows how the organization works. With the main structure identified, an expert analysis can start to fill in some of the unknowns.

The lifecycle of an issue

By studying similar issues that have gained momentum or lost steam, you can start to predict the potential parameters of a covert threat as it emerges. And as you gain a better understanding of those behind the threat, you can assess their threshold for sticking with it and exploit specific vulnerabilities that sap their zeal.

Audience growth

You can see if an audience is starting to assemble around a specific topic or location, how that might align with past threats and what its growth pattern might portend for future activity.

Competitor Footprint

Tracking activity from its start and then following its progression—in relation to both your company and similar organizations—can help assess whether you're a primary target or incidental to the cause. You might think everyone is out to get you, when in reality the unknown antagonist cares far more about someone else.

Geo-location analysis

When you do become aware of public interactions, you can place a lens over the event or channel to gain critical intelligence about the potential antagonist and its supporters—perhaps even enough to drag them out of the shadows.

Ultimately, the combination of Audience Architecture, threat analysts and expert investigators could allow you to walk into the corporate boardroom and explain how an emerging antagonist will likely proceed and what actions the company might take to prevent or combat the threat. You'll know these antagonists as well as any competitor you study. If you categorize and conduct the right online analysis of the issues that matter to your company, you can track virtually anyone who associates with the issue at hand—and perpetually learn from activity on related topics that might emerge in the future. It's the best intuition model you can create in today's world. For such a critical issue, anything short of this type of effort is unacceptable.

UNDERSTANDING OUR OPPOSITION

By Cindy Storer, a veteran intelligence analyst in the war on al-Qa'ida,
having worked it since the early 1990s. Since leaving CIA in 2007, Cindy teaches
for John's Hopkins University; consults for the International Spy Museum and
speaks on data, analysis and counterterrorism to various audiences.
She was featured in the UK television show, "Hunted."

Comparing business threats to terrorism is extreme, but terrorism analysts don't just look at the terrorists. To understand threats, they look at all kinds of opposition groups with similar grievances and goals and at the societies in which they operate. This is because people don't become terrorists overnight, terrorist groups don't form in a moment, and few terrorist plots can be carried out without connection to the broader society.

As Mao Tse-Tung said, "The guerrilla must move amongst the people as a fish swims in the sea." That sea, like social media and the Web as a whole, is mostly full of perfectly harmless fish, but no one wants to be stung by a jellyfish much less eaten by a shark.

These different kinds of threats are not always easy to spot, or to separate from each other. Take the situation in Syria today. The vast majority of people are just trying to survive, often fleeing to neighboring countries. In the battles are people: just trying to defend their homes and families, seeking vengeance, trying to overthrow the government, and trying to fundamentally change society and the people themselves through force. Its these last who tend to be the terrorists. This is the goal of the Islamic State (IS or ISIS).

We have learned through long experience that it is essential to tell these groups apart and treat them in different ways. Ignoring or suppressing legitimate grievances for too long leads to frustration, too much frustration leads some to anger, and anger can lead some to rage, especially if they feel they are being attacked. That causes most threats. Why make worse enemies when you don't have to? But then there are those who want to destroy you for their own reasons, like ISIS, and that requires a whole different approach.

Regardless, standard positive messaging that is all about you will not have a positive effect on them. The United States made this mistake after 9/11 by hiring a Madison Avenue marketer to develop positive messages about the US to be shown in Middle Eastern countries. They failed miserably to make even a dent in negative views of the US. People need positive messages about themselves, and how their life can be better.

So how do we tell the threats apart, learn what approach will work best for each, and find the most threatening actors who are hiding in the shadows? Before the 1990s, this was accomplished through police work, surveys, and living within communities. Now, everyone is online in one form or another. We can 'see' groups and networks, and how they form, change, and dissolve, by mapping connections. We can read their press, see if what they are saying to each other is different, and see if what they are doing matches their words. And we can see which groups are related to which, and how. Not perfectly, but with much greater specificity than ever before.

Chapter 15

MODERN DAY ISSUES MANAGEMENT

*"Real knowledge
is to know the
extent of one's
ignorance."*

- Confucius

I broke into the communications industry in 1985 with Carl Byoir & Associates, the industry's third largest firm at the time. This firm knew how to prepare for a crisis. We would analyze the top three to five troubling scenarios for clients, prepare five to 10 pages of questions and answers and combine it all in a crisis binder geared to anticipate almost any potential issue. The binders looked wonderful on the shelves, where they gathered dust. We rarely used more than three to five questions and answers, and no more than one statement was especially useful. Basically, it was a lot of work to prepare for things that might never happen—a Napoleonic Complex in communications.

The variety of crises I've worked on in the years since have shaped my approach. A case of anthrax in New York City; a terrorist attack in Paris; Mad Cow Disease; the world's largest battery recall—you learn a lot when you live inside these types of crises. And what I've come to understand through all of them is that, with today's technology, we can be as proficient in shaping the world's view of a negative story as we are in shaping a positive one. We truly can anticipate, prepare for and succeed with our issues-management strategies by learning from the clues that appear right in front of us.

> We know how customers will find our story via search, so we can use the right language to make it easier to find the good side than the bad.

As I discussed in the prior chapter, Audience Architecture can work as an online security system that helps us combat our brands' antagonists. In much the same way, we can deploy it for modern-day issues management more broadly. In dire circumstances, it can help us drive our story by finding allies who will share our side. We can identify the channels that really shape the conversation, so we can put together the right offense and defense alike. We know how customers will find our story via search, so we can use the right language to make it easier to find the good side than the bad. The principles are remarkably straightforward.

- We juxtapose negative news and content flow against our normal, positive customer audience, so we can identify present or future overlaps.

- We examine the human behavior of critics so we can anticipate their next moves. We're no longer anticipating which Q&As to write; we're anticipating when and where to deploy Twitter, Facebook, video and other social-media responses in real time— down to a small handful of key influencers.

- We know how our audience consumes media, so we can understand the differences in what they learn and know. And we can reach them directly because we know their public social footprint.

CATEGORIZING ISSUES AND INCIDENTS

We can also lean on Audience Architecture to better categorize the issues and incidents that can generate the most problems for a brand. We can see what topics are most common, what questions are most frequently asked, what basic protective measures we should take and the key lessons learned from past crises. People always follow patterns, with issues as well as anything else:

1. *The top ten topics at a typical company.* Most companies share a similar set of core issues that can arise—trademark and intellectual property disputes; product litigation; product crises; environmental/advocacy crises; advertising deemed offensive; shareholder concerns; the rogue employee/leaked confidential information; rumors; crises with products; and negative customer experience.

2. *The 77 questions asked about issues.* We know from the work conducted by Vincent T. Covello that journalists ask a common set of 77 questions when reporting on an issue. Thus, we know what journalists most frequently write about. So in many cases, journalists on the scene act as our "issue influencer group." According to Covello's research, "Journalists are likely to ask six questions in a crisis (who, what, where, when, why, how) that relate to three broad topics: one, what happened; two, what caused it to happen; and three, what does it mean?"

3. *Basic Protective Measures.* The best way to develop protective measures is to think like the person or thing that could cause harm. What would they do or how would that occur?

A CALL AND RESPONSE OF THREAT SCENARIOS

As we prepare our issues-management strategies and tactics, it often helps to role-play threat scenarios and responses to them. I'll go through several here, but please note that most of these can and should be customized for the brands and topics specific to your company.

The Antagonist: I would buy websites and start social channels with sub-domains that mention your brand or campaign, and then use them against you. I'll start sites with your brand as the URL in certain countries, and then load them with all our arguments. Then, I'll buy your keywords and drive people to our site.

- **Our Response:** Our key step is to identify and lock up the available uniform resource locators (URLs) and the top 100 sub-domains for the widest range of social channels we can imagine for our brand and campaigns. This will also help us combat spammers, who routinely buy sites and get sub-domains to steal traffic that should be going to our sites.

I'm going to find your weakest link and enter your company through that place. It might be your Facebook page in Vietnam or your Twitter account for selling used equipment. I don't care. I just need one opening, and then I'll camp out inside your corporate firewalls and see what I can find.

- What we will do is build a central repository that has the passwords and user IDs for every website and every social channel for every country we do business in. Going country by country, we will do a clean sweep of all our brands' websites and social channels, deleting those we don't need. And we'll ensure that all of these sites and channels—including those of our agencies and contractors—are managed to the security standards of our IT department.

If I am writing a story about your company or brand on this issue, I'm going to use search to find out more before I call you.

- We need to do the top 100 search queries about our brand and the potential issues we will face. We use this to determine what someone would learn if they did any of these queries, and then create a search plan that will get our story in all of the right places over time.

If I don't like you and I had success giving you a hard time before, I'm going to follow a similar path to raise hell the next time.

- So what we do is study the habits of all of our antagonists, in aggregate—and then individually, if appropriate—so we can see what the likely courses of action will be and plan for them.

If I don't like you, I'm triggered by some topics more than others.

- We can figure out the words and phrases that set you off and simply stop using them.

When I prepare to go after a brand or company, I'll talk to a few friends and whip my online community into a frenzy.

- We can often put in alert systems to identify emerging crises before they hit the press. If the first time we deal with an issue occurs when the press calls, we've missed an opportunity to nip it in the bud. More than 90% of issues are known and chronic; there are few major surprises in life.

If I am trying to bait you into an argument, I'm hoping you'll react like a stereotypical company, taking a long time to respond, talking in corporate voice polished by lawyers and sharing too much information in your statements.

- We realize that when we comment early on an emerging issue, we often can slow down or even stop the argument. If a true antagonist comes out to get us, then it's all the more imperative that we speak as real people, with quick and focused responses. We'll be real.

Once the issue is contained, you'll forget about it and go back to your normal business. And when you do, all the negatives I poured into the online world will remain in search engines and your issue will continue to smolder.

- Sorry, we already know we have to look at our top 100 search queries after an issue dies down, and we'll proceed to get our side of the story into each one of those. We will push the negatives down and off the top screens.

This issue is important to me. I'll just keep poking at you whenever it makes sense, gathering new information that I can use against you.

- We won't increase the chances of this happening, because we'll identify the topic's 50 biggest influencers and, with another algorithm, figure out the top four influencers for each of those top 50. We can then shape the attitudes of the top influencers, but also the influencers' of those influencers. We might not change your mind, or that of other antagonists, but we can change the ecosystem around them.

I know you hate saying you were ever wrong, so I'll be sure people know you won't.

- We will humbly say we're sorry if we screw up, but we won't apologize simply to placate our critics.

I know that rumors take on a life of their own, so I'll breathe life into as many of them as I can.

- We know this, too, but through our tracking system we can recognize them early and respond immediately. Most people who start rumors do so out of ignorance, not malevolence.

We can make it appear as if dozens or hundreds of people will descend upon your event, elevating your fears that something could happen.

- We can place a lens over any part of the earth, including our event, and see what is really happening. This does not fool us anymore.

Getting thousands or tens of thousands of people to sign a petition or retweet something freaks you out, so I'll do that.

- We understand that slacktivism is a new form of advocacy, but we also know it has exceptionally low impact. Many people will touch a screen to show support, but they rarely know what they are supporting and almost never follow-up.

Whenever you thwart me in my mother tongue, I'll raise my issues in other languages.

- We track languages that follow the definition of mutual intelligibility. So if you create an issue in Czech, we can look at Polish and Slovak at the same time. We know people gravitate toward languages that resemble their native tongue.

We can role-play issues all day long and still miss contingencies. But the sheer depth and breadth of insight from Audience Architecture can help us adapt to unforeseen issues and give us the information we need to create issues-management strategies on the fly. And because we can see the habits, trends and demand for a controversial issue like never before, we can protect our companies and brands in a far more effective way—even when surprises do erupt.

Or we can keep doing exhaustive Q&As, standby statements and binders. After all, they do look pretty on the shelf.

SPEED, PREPARATION AND THE EVERLASTING POWER OF THE TRUTH

By Lord Chadlington, founder and head of two major communications companies – Shandwick (now Weber Shandwick) and Huntsworth. A member of the House of Lords, Peter has served as an advisor for several Prime Ministers, including PM John Major and PM David Cameron and as a fellow or director for many important aspects of British culture, including Chairman of the Royal Opera House. He also recently collaborated on a novel, *Head of State*, with BBC TV political presenter Andrew Marr.

Those first minutes, even seconds, are crucial to managing any crisis in the modern age. Consider, for example, the photos and video on a mobile phone. The initial photograph taken on the site of an industrial accident, or the short video of the chairman answering a stockholder's question at the annual meeting, can set the tone for every message that follows. From that moment on, as that photo or video goes viral you fall further onto the back foot. And the slower you react, the less likely you will ever regain the momentum and, with it, the authority to manage the story proactively.

In the media frenzy that accompanies any crisis, that opening moment sets the tenor for the whole communications program. That first picture, so often taken by an independent person who's seen as having no real agenda, will be considered 100% credible. It will become the lasting image as the crisis plays out, a touchstone for all that follows. Just think of the photo of 3-year-old Alan Kurdi, who died in the Mediterranean Sea while trying to migrate from Syria with his father. Reflect on the impact of that one picture – if you've seen it, you'll never forget it. It made some of the most powerful politicians in the world change policies and spurred ordinary citizens to their checkbooks, homes and hearts.

A crisis gives you little time to prepare. By definition you do not know when it will come, how hard it will hit and how long it will last. Of course, some preparation is possible, particularly setting strategy and employing people senior enough to make decisions and stick by them. Role playing, testing our response technology and keeping everything fresh and in highest level of working order is the minimum threshold of preparation we need to undertake.

Remember two things: First, good managers excel in crises and show their true mettle; and second, it's always the cover up that kills the company or unseats the president, not the original disaster.

The key in every crisis, then, is to tell the truth. Do not have the truth beaten out of you. Get there first with the full, honest story. It will make the crisis pass more quickly, and you will emerge in better shape. The truth is all.

Chapter 16

THE SHIFT FROM REPUTATION TO RELEVANCE

"The most important thing in communication is hearing what isn't said."

- Peter Drucker

ary Grates and I had just finished a consultation about corporate reputation with a Fortune 500 client. As we walked outside where we could talk freely, Gary, a W2O colleague who has dedicated most of his professional life to reputation, change management, employee communications and all things that shape the "being" of a company, was animated. "I gotta tell you, it's no longer about reputation," he said. "Reputation doesn't mean the same thing anymore. It's about relevance. Are you relevant to the people who matter to your company? And how do you know? The (communications) industry is looking at this the wrong way."

Gary, as usual, was spot on. By that time, we'd conducted corporate reputation reviews for dozens of clients over the course of years, but we'd adopted a different twist to them. We knew our clients' customers didn't fall neatly into groups that care about amorphous topics like financial strength, pipeline or sustainability. From our work with influencers in the general public, we knew we had to build algorithms that look at hundreds of variables, not 10 or 20 topics organized neatly in a pie chart.

Yet most reputational research has missed the mark for years now. As a consumer of this research when I sat on the client side, I felt this intuitively, but I couldn't prove it. Now, we could, and as Gary noted after our briefing, we realized we should pay more attention to corporate relevance, and less to corporate reputation.

RELEVANCE: HOW TOPICS CONNECT, HOW WE LEARN ABOUT THEM, HOW WE JUSTIFY OUR BELIEFS

When companies first started measuring reputation, they did it in a very controlled media world. You needed to be ranked in the top 100 lists published by certain magazines. You could place newspaper ads in key markets to tell people what you believed. You could give speeches and declare new campaigns to strengthen your position externally, helping heighten awareness of your values and interests. Those lovely pie charts would prove your brilliance!

What we never knew in the 1970s—and even up to the early 2000s— was whether anyone really cared. We could measure awareness and the audience's ability to remember a campaign. And when people ran harmless campaigns, consumers would say they were basically OK with what we'd done, which to us always sounded like a Sally Field acceptance speech—"You like me! You really, really like me!"

The advent of social media destroyed those delusions. We now see everyone online—all three billion or more—and we know whether they love us, hate us, or really couldn't care less. If a company's initiatives help the consumer, they'll jump on board. If it rubs them the wrong way, they'll say so. But if a campaign holds no relevance to their lives, the initiatives won't even hit the edge of their radar screen. Sometimes that doesn't matter. A brand, product or initiative simply might not fit certain consumers' lives. But for the customers it could touch, a company or brand has to prove its relevance to their lives.

RELEVANCE: NINE INSIGHTS ABOUT RELEVANCE AND REPUTATION

Because corporate reputation can be such a sensitive matter for most companies, I'll avoid going into any specific examples here. But by scrutinizing our clients' experiences and our research base, we've identified nine key insights that conveniently enough, give us our RELEVANCE framework.

Reality opens minds and creates opportunities for a company to evolve

When we look at the companies global media outlets track the closest, we find a fascinating commonality. The reporters and bloggers who report a company's every move rarely shape its reputation for the rest of the world. One finds little overlap between those who write the news story on a company's financial results and those who care about a company's commitment to sustainability or innovation or other initiatives important to their core customers.

Why does this happen so consistently? It turns out our reporters cover larger companies because they have to cover them and they report, essentially, to the financial markets. Compared with the consumer population of the U.S., let alone the world, a miniscule fraction of people work in the financial markets or watch CNBC all day.

Meanwhile, the company should focus on what they do to accelerate innovation, sustainability or some other initiative that resonates with customers. If Company X is innovating in packaging design, then bloggers, forum posters and influential journalists who track package-design innovation will love to hear everything the firm can share. Make the story too broad or too big, though, and no one will care. We need to find what realities matter to our target audience, and use that knowledge to craft our message, our story and our actions.

Employees are the most untapped resource for building relevance

When we think of larger companies with 50,000 to 200,000 employees, we're talking about the population of a midsize U.S. city. If we think of our employee population as a city, we start to understand the influence it can have. Each town will have a mayor and a city council, who collectively steer the conversation. So when we think of building relevance in the market, we have to think about relevance both inside and outside our company—and who guides the message in both domains. Employees inhabit both worlds and can impact both, yet most companies don't take the time to identify their mayors and council members (i.e. their internal influencers). Rather, firms share all their news top-down and hope it cascades to people who will share it. That rarely goes well.

> Identify what various employees passionately care about and allow them to lead both internal and external conversations on those topics.

Try this instead: Identify what various employees passionately care about and allow them to lead both internal and external conversations on those topics. Let your engineers and designers talk about their packaging innovations, and make their discussion a centerpiece of how you communicate. Feature those leaders in your external blogs, so customers know you walk the talk.

Listen to the people who matter, not those awarding random trophies

Didn't you win enough accolades in Little League or school? Even if you didn't, I'm sure you quickly realized that most of them are little more than a nice pat on the back. Their importance wears off almost immediately. In business, identifying the audiences important to your company and understanding what they care about matters. You don't care what the world thinks. The accolades don't matter. You care about what your customers and your target audience think and do every day. And companies can construct corporate reputation platforms that listen to audiences and flag the stories most relevant to them—once again, Audience Architecture and Storytizing going hand-in-hand. If you know what your customer base cares about, you can deliver the right story directly to them.

Do rankings matter? Of course they do, but because they differ from awards and trophies, people, including your customers, are conditioned to watch and believe in those who receive a ranking. Not all rankings matter—like other aspects of reputation—but you can now see which rankings exert influence on your target audiences, concentrate on those and not waste your time with the rest.

When I worked at Novartis, we did this type of analysis before all of the technology existed that we have today. We were still able to figure out that 43 rankings really mattered to us, with 22 of them being quantitative and 21 being qualitative. It really helped us focus our efforts.

Edges in the market are where you make a difference

If you look at a company with a dozen products, five strategic initiatives, a global footprint and a few other moving parts, its various levers of relevance carry varying degrees of power. With Audience Architecture algorithms, we can spot your edge or potential edges. This is where to spend your time.

Too often, we keep talking about the same, tired campaign year after year because we've declared it a corporate priority. We'll say we care deeply about the community, which is why we contribute to groups that support those issues. Yet, if we look closer, we find that 10 people in that community are major influencers, whom we ought to invite to post on our blog and come into our world. We can find the one untapped issue that our customers feel is highly important, but is ignored by our competitors. We can create new channels for previously disconnected groups to discuss the issues they all care deeply about.

The edges we need in the market sit right in front of us if we take time to watch and hear what our audience says and does.

The edges we need in the market sit right in front of us if we take time to watch and hear what our audience says and does. They don't become obvious if we stare at PowerPoint slides that tell us: "Elites are 3% more favorable towards our company and how it innovated in Q2 versus Q1." Get out of the slide decks and into reality—go find your edge.

Voice of a company matters, much like how we talk with each other

We spend a lot of time trying to get into the mythical voice of the CEO when we share corporate updates. Many of us get quite good at it. To be authentic and relevant, however, you have to learn what the CEO really cares about, what he or she is doing, what people want to hear and with whom he or she speaks. It's a lot harder than guessing at the CEO's interests, language and tone. When we do the similar hard work to identify what the audience cares about our latest initiative, we tend to remove all the varnish and focus on what they really want to hear, from whom they want to hear it—often not the C-Suite—and where they would prefer to have the conversation. This voice alignment takes a huge step towards greater relevance.

Audience is our clue machine

As I've noted throughout this book, you have to know your audience's preferences to reach them effectively. But to do that, you also have to architect your audience and not rely on something off the shelf. Precision matters, and relying on old audience segmentation to target your message will leave some customers interested, some bored and some altogether annoyed. Build the right Audience Architecture from the foundation up.

Negatives are the storm clouds in the distance

Texans have a saying: "If you don't like the weather, wait 10 minutes." Even when it looks sunny, the negatives always lurk somewhere just off the business horizon. If they haven't arrived yet, wait 10 minutes. So we have to ask whether we're tracking our negative audience effectively, taking the time and effort to understand what they care about, what patterns of behavior they display and whether we can educate, outsmart or outwork them.

With today's technologies, we can track these individuals or groups, research their past behavior and predict their most-likely future actions. We now have an alert system, a smart filter that gives us definitive information about what topics matter to the critics and how they react to various topical messages. I truly believe that the more a company learns about the people who don't like it, the better it can align its brands and messages to build greater relevance and understanding. We can prepare for the storm.

Consistency of behavior is more important than consistency of message

Both matter, but if you broadcast the most consistent messages in the world but don't follow up your behavior, you lose. If you have perfect message points but you don't fully resonate with your influencers, you sub-optimize. Today's always-online audiences take note of our behavior at all times. Do we participate in their communities at the same pace and level that they do? Do we stick around when it benefits them more than us, or drop content bombs when convenient to us? Do we ever let our guard down and speak as real people? And how many key influencers have we met in person, invited to an event or followed on our social channels?

People know who's consistent and worth paying attention to, and they tune out those who just sell the stories they were paid to sell.

Ecosystem of an audience judges us better than anyone

Crowdsourcing can generate business lessons that our sophisticated research often overlooks. The customers who judge our reputation often take their cues from crowds. So who do they listen to? Typically, they follow a combination of certain journalists, certain thought leaders in a particular area and employees who share their take with the public.

We need to watch, listen and reach out through the Audience Architecture platform, which reveals relevance on a real-time basis.

But to pinpoint the influencers, we need to watch, listen and reach out through the Audience Architecture platform, which reveals relevance on a real-time basis. As a result, you'll develop new performance indicators that show how stakeholder groups influence each other over time, ultimately hurting or benefitting your company.

When Gary and I stepped out of that client's office and he talked plainly about the power of relevance over reputation, this is the precise audience alignment he was talking about. We had been consumers of reputational research for decades, but we now realized companies had missed the real picture—that building relevance was inseparable from driving reputational value. Technological advances have given us the listening device we never realized we needed. Listen closely, and you can learn what's relevant every time.

Chapter 17

EMPLOYEES, THE UNTAPPED NATURAL RESOURCE

*"An employee
who's one of hundreds,
rather than one of a few,
is unlikely to feel
personally responsible for
helping the organization
adapt and change."*

- Gary Hamel

Over the years, I've listened to Ram Charan, Gary Hamel and many of the other top management experts expound on the importance of organizational excellence. They're brilliant consultants, and they've helped the Fortune 500 beyond measure, but I always felt a nagging concern as I listened to them and tried to put their admonitions into practice. When I look at 100,000 employees inside a company, I see 100,000 souls. I see 1,000 tribes who care deeply about specific topics or functions. I don't see a group of 100,000 people just waiting to be told what to do, expecting them to cascade the information through their direct reports and ensure everyone falls into line. I know I've never felt like a grunt waiting for my marching orders—or when I did feel like that, I certainly didn't like it.

We don't roll that way, and we never have. There's never been any reason to think a CEO letter or internal campaign will lead to great success. Companies have to take a distinctly different tack from traditional practices, one that only became possible after the technology developments of recent years. Company leaders have to align with employees by understanding what they think and what they do, both externally and internally.

If they don't get it internally, employees will seek outside validation and, in search of it, will share their thinking outside the workplace. (They, too, follow the 1-9-90 model, so tracking a set of influential employees can provide a view of broader trends, excitement and dissatisfaction within your company.) And while employees have many justifications to stay with or leave their employer, they only have a handful of reasons to seek outside validation of their work.

1. *Lack of an outlet.* Yes, the big bosses can always send an email or a new video with a few perfectly crafted messages. But if I am in the middle of the organization, where can I express myself freely and learn from my peers without interference or overbearing oversight? If I can't find that forum internally, I take it outside and express my ideas in forums, blogs and social channels.

2. *Am I rewarded fairly?* Every company tells me I am, but how do I know? I need to ask my friends and my peer communities to help me figure it out. Employees will always wonder, regardless of career stage.

3. *How will I get my next job?* The average worker will change jobs seven to 10 times over the course of his or her career, so it becomes increasingly important to keep in touch with peers outside of work. If you are a software programmer, designer or an accountant, you build your network of similar workers and workplaces, because it

can help you with what comes next. And since we often do this via public networking sites, it makes it easier for search firms to find us and accelerate job shifts.

4. *No one cares about me.* If I am always being talked to, I feel underappreciated. We feel much more appreciated when we have a chance to express our ideas. Whether done internally or externally, the worker receives some form of validation in return. Why not keep those potentially valuable insights within the company? If you don't allow discussion and dissent inside your walls, your employees will take the conversation elsewhere.

5. *Bad management.* If you feel overworked, micromanaged or don't admire your boss, you'll keep your eyes and ears open. Opportunities for advancement seem far less likely when you perceive your boss as bad or even mediocre, even if you have the wrong read on him or her.

Employees can count on these tribes like an extended family, and regularly feel more affinity to these groups than to their employers. It's about relationships, open-minded thinking, counsel and knowledge.

PRECOMMERCE FOR EMPLOYEES

Thanks to technology advances, our employees can easily seek and find validation with new tribes of professionals who willingly share ideas, listen to and teach each other, and build a relationship that's often far stronger than any connection inside the organization. Think of this as

PreCommerce for employees. How much time do your employees spend learning, sharing, educating and even training from outside sources you don't know about? How much influence do their tribes have on their next move? What reputation do your company and your brands have within these tribes?

The professional tribes that our employees communicate with are their rock. They consistently provide help, and they evolve as the employee does throughout their entire career. Employees can count on these tribes like an extended family, and regularly feel more affinity to these groups than to their employers. It's about *relationships, open-minded thinking, counsel* and *knowledge.* As a result, we have built a new model for recruitment, retention and employee change management that is centered on these four areas.

THE VARIABLES THAT INFLUENCE EMPLOYEES

Companies make plenty of outright errors, but when we think of employee engagement it helps to think not of what they do wrong, but what they don't do well enough. Many companies rely on an annual employee survey, informal focus groups or other infrequent actions to gauge employees' views on their company, their job or their department. That information often gets generalized even further, so it ends up fitting a macro view of what to do inside the company. But in my view, that approach has never had much impact. If an employee doesn't see any value in responding—of if they suspect superiors will use negative answers against them—why even respond? And those who do respond often give answers that fit what the company believes is important, rather than how they truly think and act.

Today. . .we can see exactly
what our employees share
professionally and, to a great
extent, personally as well.

Today, though, we can see exactly what our employees share professionally and, to a great extent, personally as well. They post ideas and thoughts in all forms of media, reaching out to virtual peer groups worldwide. They make decisions based on the relevance of the company to the outside world, all influenced by a network broader than just their immediate colleagues. If we want to understand how our employee morale stacks up against the overall marketplace—in terms of passion, knowledge and peer influence—we have to start by outlining the following variables:

1. *Type of Employee.* If we look at engineers, for example, we want to break down their areas of interest based on the tribes with which they align. If we look at what the company is building, we can now figure out the languages, communities and areas of passion which apply.

    a. Specific programming languages — The top 10 are Java, C, C++, Python, C#, R, PHP, JavaScript, Ruby, Matlab.

    b. Specific communities — These range from the Apache Software Foundation to Ubuntu Foundation to SourceForge.

    c. Areas of passion — From digital rights management to software security to standards.

2. *Tribes* — We can determine the tribes our employees naturally hang out with to learn, share ideas and build their professional mindset. To ascertain whether our company is part of a larger tribal conversation that will strengthen our retention and recruitment efforts, we need to look at three layers of influence.

    a. Inside Influencers — Who is influential inside our company on each key topic?

b. Inside/Out Influencers — Which of our employee influencers is influential in the external world and, with the right tools and resources, could be influential inside as well?

c. Category Influencers — In each topic category, who are the experts with whom we don't have a relationship but should?

3. *Location* — We want to understand the location of various influencers, because their proximity can have a positive or negative effect on our game plan. For example, if your key cities contain large influencer communities, the ability for employees to move to a new company increases. You can judge your ability to recruit and retain, but three types of influencers carry more weight with employees.

a. Virtual team — People who share and learn together, regardless of geography. They're interested in the broader category and are passion-driven. They participate to further the cause. Open-source software is a classic example of this.

b. In-house team plus external — Where are your influential employees located? You might have officers in five hub cities for software engineers. But when you look at location, you see that your Silicon Valley teams do all the talking and sharing, while your London, New York, Beijing and Sao Paulo teams say little to nothing. That's not a good mix.

c. Location-based — Who is an active part of the technology community in a city? Knowing who has deep local connections can give you an avenue to effectively reach new recruits and ensure your company is well known in the right circles.

ALIGNING INTERNAL AND EXTERNAL COMMUNITIES

We can know who exerts the greatest influence on each area of expertise and where they hold sway. Armed with that external information, we can adjust some of our most important internal communications. We now check our soft variables—the internal topics the company considers crucial to its culture and business, such as women in technology, work-life balance or carpooling—and then we look for the points at which our internal and external communities align.

Tipping Points

Companies need to identify the tribes related to their business, figure out what each one cares about and rank those concerns. We want to know what resonates, whether from a professional perspective or in relation to these soft variables. So we add these soft variables to our Audience Architecture analysis, revealing what resonates publicly and how it ties to the views of our employee tribes. What returns is a dose of truth—a radar system that shows what our employees really care about, what their communities care about and how aligned those concerns are with our version of corporate reality. From there, we can start to get increasingly fancy, perhaps matching up recruitment and attrition in the same way that we would measure sales results and marketing initiatives.

Recruitment and Attrition by Tribe

If we look at recruitment and attrition through the lens of the tribe, we can see whether market factors influence employees' decisions to join or leave the firm. We might start to notice that expertise in certain software languages correlates with more volatility in our workforce, because those skills are in high demand and tight supply. Or we might discover emerging technologies that put a premium on new skills, forcing us to add talent as soon as possible—similar to how Elastic Search exploded onto the tech scene years ago.

THE ROCK MODEL

As managers work to align their internal and external communities and communications, four straightforward principles can help guide us toward greater synergy between people inside and outside the company. I call these the ROCK model—the key factors that make for better retention, recruitment and company morale:

- *Relationships* — Are we building the right relationships with our own employee influencers as well as external influencers? Do we support the right groups?

- *Open-minded thinking* — Are we willing to hear the truth and realize when our interests and efforts don't align with those of our own employees? Will we do something about it?

- *Counsel* — Are we willing and able to take the advice that we receive when we listen to external communities? Do we seek more information and ask questions to learn from our own employees?

- *Knowledge* — Have we empowered our employees to expand our collective knowledge and teach the company what is relevant inside and outside our walls?

EMPOWERING THE INFLUENCER NETWORK

We know who creates relevant content inside a company. We know what the relevant market cares about. And we know where and to what degree these internal and external communities align. Now we can use that insight to develop our influencer network and content strategy in a way that capitalizes on the common interest and passions of both sides.

The Blogger Network

The content we discuss or ought to discuss internally—and who can lead those conversations—becomes apparent through the ROCK model and Audience Architecture. So now we want to empower the influential employees who can create and share content on the topics that align our internal content strategy with the external world. After determining what an ideal blogger network looks like, we can train and help curate initial posts to set this in motion. Eventually, as team members get more confident about internal blog posts, we have them to start sharing publicly, as well.

> When we acknowledge internally what we learn from the outside, we heighten our credibility with employees and customers alike.

Content Strategy

Since we also identified both the professional topics and soft variables that matter to our company, employees and customers, we know what resonates. This leads to a new pathway to discuss key initiatives or study attrition patterns and contrast that information with external variables. And when we acknowledge internally what we learn from the outside, we heighten our credibility with employees and customers alike.

Continual Feedback Mechanisms

We put in place an idea community so all engineers and all employees can quickly and easily share their ideas for improving the company and its products. Throw out the surveys. Give employees chances to vote on ideas, comment on proposals, and then aggregate the results to gain insight you can integrate into future development efforts. In essence, tap into your teams' stream of consciousness. Then go a step further and ask employees to sign up and share content online. If an employee willingly provides his or her social media handle for company purposes, providing them some basic training and content will give them added credibility and influence with outside audiences.

Companies that empower their internal tribes and external influencers will see the real, self-reinforcing power of today's new-media platforms. We can reach communities that matter through earned and shared media. We can sharply reduce our reliance on paid media. Our recruitment costs drop. We align with our employees and reduce churn. And when we don't agree, we know why and can provide our best argument for our beliefs.

We no longer have an excuse to treat employees with anything less than the respect we give our most powerful outside influencers. We can identify and understand their tribes and empower them to drive their passion and, when done right, our passions as well.

FROM BROADCAST TO CONVERSATION: THE NEW EMPLOYEE ENGAGEMENT

Gary Grates is one of the world's leaders in understanding how organizations communicate, teach and empower their employees to shape their future. He has worked for CEOs of many Fortune 500 companies, is a professor at Syracuse University for the Center for Social Commerce and a member of the Arthur W. Page Society.

In today's content-rich, attention-challenged organization, gaining and retaining employee interest and engagement is crucial to survival and growth. It starts with a knowledgeable and aware workforce, from top executives to the newest entry-level employee.

Organizational communications has evolved to a new level, helping companies build this more-engaged workforce. Communications now accelerate the pace of decision making, challenge people's knowledge and provide information that leaders, managers and employees can use to frame arguments, illustrate situations, make decisions and launch initiatives. It's no longer a broadcast or top-down model, but one based on dialogue, discussion, and debate. It's about making things personal, so people can make the arguments themselves.

But haven't employees always been critical to business success?

EMPLOYEES ARE THE ENTERPRISE'S AUTHENTIC EXPERTS

The familiar refrain, "Employees are your most important asset," certainly was understood by many business leaders. Unfortunately, too many managers compromise on that belief when the marketplace gets difficult. And that oversight gets infinitely more troubling in today's Storytizing world.

First, nothing stays inside the company anymore. In the social and digital reality of today, what happens inside a company is visible to the external audience. Employees can be your greatest advocates or your worst critics. And what they say carries tremendous credibility. Regardless of position or tenure, employees are seen as the real "voice" inside an organization - a voice that now has more avenues for expression than ever before. Providing workers with information in the form of stories, stats and visual content allows them to act on your behalf in their social spheres, thus extending the company's relevance and efficacy.

Secondly, the means by which we, as communicators, operate has grown exponentially. It starts with analytics - no longer can we cite instinct or our gut reactions when planning and executing communications inside the organization. Today, analytics can discern a range of factors:

- Employee archetypes as a means to gauge tone, content, context, cadence, and frequency

- Internal networks of influence

- Information habits

- Use and effectiveness of platforms

- Content and format acceptance and amplification

- Knowledge of strategic priorities and imperatives

- Areas of concern impacting retention

Put succinctly, analytics that lead to insight have forever changed how we approach organizational effectiveness. So in shaping internal communication as a means for improving our effectiveness, we have to consider several new tenets:

1. The CEO ultimately drives employee behavior and the organization's culture. A clear, well-articulated guiding principle (whether about culture, company goals or values) can help focus an organization, align and motivate employees and guide effective internal communications.

2. Stories capture interest and ignite passion. People react to stories that place things in context, make things personal and relate the premise to their experiences. Organizations that can bring strategy and marketplace realities to life through storytelling will win in this new era.

3. Decision-making must be inclusive and integrated. A perceived lack of involvement in organizational decision-making leaves employees feeling disillusioned and disempowered. We must shape communications as a tool for linking employees to business decisions, creating a channel for them to voice opinions and suggestions that ultimately will affect business outcomes.

4. View employees as a public constituency not a captive audience. Traditionally, most leaders, managers and communicators treated employees as a captive audience and to a lesser extent, a necessary burden.

The new world for organizational communications and employee engagement presents unique challenges and opportunities. Done right, we can make a quantum leap from necessary function to critical organizational priority.

Chapter 18
INNOVATION THAT MATTERS

"Every act of creation is first of all an act of destruction."

– Pablo Picasso

We all read the same news articles and books about famous inventors. Whether it is Jobs or Edison or Zuckerberg, they seem far removed from the rest of us. How could we ever invent something at this scale? We probably never will, but we always have small opportunities to innovate and make a difference for ourselves, our communities and our organizations. We need to take a look at what exists today and, as Picasso would put it, begin that initial process of destruction of the model, service or product we feel we can improve. It's a healthy dissatisfaction with the status quo that leads to creating the next model.

Most innovation is incremental, so it can be difficult to figure out the areas ripest for change. I think about it constantly—it's a fundamental requirement of my job—so I'll share a few examples here. In each, I'll also try to lay out how my colleagues and I brainstormed and tested new ideas we launched for each sector.

MARKET TRANSFORMATION IN HEALTHCARE

The 2010 Affordable Care Act has completely changed how we'll seek care, how we're insured and the pricing of treatment throughout the healthcare market. Like any transformation, this one has built up pressure for every industry directly—and most industries indirectly—related to health and medicine. It represents a far-reaching act of creative destruction over a 10- to 20-year period, all in the spirit of improving care.

Regardless of your opinion about the law, it has undoubtedly opened up an era of innovation and opportunity in these industries. As we approached the end of 2018, we couldn't get through a week without hearing about a new digital health service, a new mobile app or any one of hundreds of companies forming to take advantage of this volatility. This won't change any time soon, and successful ideas will have tapped into a set of steady currents that flow beneath the surface turbulence:

- *New talent is emerging* — The technology industry's best and brightest are focusing their attention on healthcare solutions, ranging from Calico (Google) to Intel and more.

- *New money is available* — Venture capital firms are setting up digital health funds separate from their existing life-science funds.

- *Every company knows the rules are changing* — No one knows exactly what the future holds, so they are willing to innovate and try new things.

- *Patients and Providers are leveraging technology faster than companies* — No one is waiting for industry to solve their problems. The consumer's urgency for a treatment and cure runs far higher than industry's urgency to solve those problems.

The magical mix of these trends leads to change. New talent, new money, new rules and customer urgency equals opportunity. And when you juxtapose that equation versus the sum of trends occurring in other, more staid industries, you can't miss the fact that health care has entered radical transformation mode.

CHANGING CONTENT CONSUMPTION HABITS

When consumers can pivot and change direction faster than we can innovate, we have another situation primed for innovation. Content consumption is one of those situations. We're already nearing 4.5 billion people connected to the Internet, pulling down blogs, photos and video across myriad digital-media channels. And in that growing cacophony, it gets harder and harder to find your audience and build a relationship with them. Yet the same technologies that drive the chaos can help us cut through it. As our devices and software improve, so do our choices and our habits:

- *Choices impact habits* — We have an ever-increasing range of choices on where we can consume content. When our choices increase, our habits change. And when our habits change, so does our audience.

- *Content changes* — As technology improves, so does the content created by any member of our peer group. If we hope to be entertained and can find new ways to do so, other choices drop off our list. Our neighbors can compete with mainstream media to capture our online attention.

- *Limited time each day* — As we seek out other ways to entertain or inform ourselves, we take time away from old habits and traditional patterns of watching and learning. We have a finite amount of time each day, so a choice to engage in one place is an opportunity lost for another—and the old usually goes out when the new arrives.

THE NEW PESO MODEL FOR MEDIA

The old PESO (paid, earned, shared, owned media) model was driven by advertising. Now, though, we're seeing a dramatic shift in which advertising is driven by the other three, resembling something more akin to an ESO-P model.

- *Earned media* — Any of us can create free media, share it on any social channel and reach the majority of our friends.

- *Shared media* — We can learn from our friends, interact with companies and even start buying products and services within certain channels.

- *Owned media* — Not much has changed. We still try to get customers to come to our websites and hope good things happen.

- *Paid media* — Paid is really about brands or companies wanting to reach you. Customers need that less than ever since they can find the information and connections they seek through earned and shared media.

BRAINSTORM AND TEST NEW IDEAS

So how did my colleagues and I at W2O approach these transformational examples?

We realized that the rapid change in the *healthcare market* will set off a blizzard of innovation, but the fundamentals won't change. Patients and their caregivers will want to learn all they can about a disease. Providers will need to access external knowledge faster, since they will probably get less from their cash-starved institutions. Insurers, government, advocates and other stakeholders in the healthcare ecosystem will take more interest than ever in reaching patients earlier, so they can prevent disease or manage it more proactively. Like any Audience Architecture and Storytizing strategy, we'll need to understand who the audience is, where they live and what they do. Then, we can inform them about new lifestyles, diets and preventative treatments that keep us all healthier. W2O built MDigitalLife to map out exactly what the health ecosystem looks like and learn from its participants every day.

> We realized we needed to create audience panels that truly represent the exact group of people a brand wants to reach, so we can understand how they change and why.

We saw a related trend in the way people *changed habits*. Every report we read came across as retrospective and out of date. Most metrics focused on one channel and told us very little about the entire digital-media and business landscape. Plus, the metrics were severely out of date. Why does anyone think a page view or an impression can still tell us anything useful? We realized we needed to create audience panels that truly represent the exact group of people a brand wants to reach, so we can understand how they change and why. We can't always predict our customers' shifting habits or preferences, but we can watch them closely enough to figure out what they need before our competitors—and often before the audience collectively realizes the shift. At W2O, we call this social graphics, and we made it a primary pillar in our Audience Architecture model.

Finally, when earned and shared become the most influential media, we have a complete *flip of the PESO model*. That means media planning will change, as will customer relationship management, research, advertising and the rest of the marketing mix. Nothing can remain sacrosanct, and at W2O we realized we needed to rebuild a system of innovation driven by three main factors:

1. *Audience Architecture* — We can identify, build and track any audience, whether B2B or B2C, with accuracy never seen before.

2. *Content Anywhere, Anytime* — We can distribute content or empower customers and employers to share it on any social channel, any form of media, any website or intranet and by email. Content now has wings.

3. *Analytics Operating System* — We automate all we can to generate timely insights that reflect the ever-changing disposition, patterns and needs of the audience.

SLOWING DOWN TIME

Athletes often experience what some of our clients and other top marketing officials have started to feel when it comes to the pace of change going on around us all. Time seems to slow down for many athletes. The ball looks bigger; the play develops more slowly. I felt it in my baseball days, especially at the plate with the bases loaded. The pitcher might be throwing a 90 MPH aspirin at the plate, but time would slow and I'd see nothing but floating beach balls coming from the mound. I didn't always succeed, but my confidence would soar and pressure would slough off. I loved those moments.

We can do the same in business if we determine what parts of the market are in our wheelhouse and attune our instincts and reflexes to work at maximum capacity. The ability to recognize a situation and act upon it become one and the same. We can open up more of those market niches with a talented and diverse team, but we can also create our own openings the more we listen, learn and react to different scenarios. We build new brainpower and mind memory to innovate. Over time, the next innovation in our zones of focus will emerge more naturally and come to us faster than our competitors.

My colleagues and I like to think of this as a "unique vision for our particular obsession." Stray too far from your areas of expertise, whether they're natural or acquired, and you go back to normal. But take heart, when company interests shift, your hard work and your keen ability to recognize, embrace and thrive upon creative destruction will bring you back into the zone.

THE TRUTH OF HOW CREATIVITY REALLY WORKS

By Mike Hartman, a Harley-Davidson riding writer and poet, who is also
Chief Creative Officer at Intouch Solutions. Mike has worked at Digitas, WPP's Chemistry
cross-agency team, and led creative at LBi's health and wellness vertical.
His work is published in industry trades (DMNews, Marketing Profs)
and leading poetry journals (Rosebud, The American Journal of Poetry).

Creative. That's a loaded word that gets people all fired up. Tell someone in marketing that you work in creative and see what reaction you get. Sure, we're all creative in our own way, but there is a method to the madness in terms of arriving at exceptional work that has the power to move a business forward. No one is going to buy from you a second time if you don't move the needle and get some stuff sold.

So the canvas is blank. It always is. Even when you're not starting from scratch. It all starts with ideas. Concepts. A vision. Barely congruous thoughts. And you don't even need to fully know how it's all going to work. But there has to be a constellation of thinking and a loose plan on how to get there. Real ideas make the difference and stand shoulders above the rest, and being able to recognize an idea from a tactic is critical. Tactics are easy. Ideas are hard. Good ideas spawn tactics like there's no tomorrow. But tactics don't always reverse engineer into amazing ideas. So we have to be relentless in our pursuit. Remarkably, technology can be a trap. It can be quite easy to mistake a buzzy bit of technology for an idea. But it isn't. It's just a way to bring a proper idea to life.

The truth is we don't always know what we want or what's best for us. And new ideas can be terrifying. Think new car designs. You hate them until you love them. It's been said that if an idea doesn't frighten you a little, there's virtually no way that it can be special or remotely transformative. So "safe" is never really all that safe. It's actually more dangerous to be safe and vanilla than it is to be risky.

First thoughts are deadly and part of the process. Just as quickly as they are conceived they need to be purged from the system so the more refined and mature thoughts can take shape. And those thoughts should be very, very simple. Often just two words. Maybe three. Purity of thought is the goal: If you cannot distill the idea down to just a few words, you're dealing with a headline. And that's another trap. Like William Carlos Williams said of poems, great lines are "machines made of words" and machines need to be built for very specific purposes. A fantastic headline is just that. A fantastic headline. But it should not be confused with an idea. Unless it actually is an idea in disguise! So strip the line naked and see what you've got.

Great work takes time. But each day we seem to have less and less of it. The only way to account for having less time is better information on the front end and to more widely test the work. Without sufficient time for work to sit and breathe, we need to call on additional resources to pressure-test the work to accelerate maturity. But there's a big difference between testing work and creation by com-mittee. To deliver breakthrough work, you have to be open to any and all feedback – but just because it's given doesn't mean it's right. Often we hear "there are no wrong ideas in brainstorms" and that's a falsehood and hedging mechanism. It may be controversial to say, but there are plenty of wrong ideas that waste a lot of time and energy. And in this business, you need all the time and energy you can get.

Chapter 19

UNLOCK INNOVATION IN YOUR ORGANIZATION

Many years ago, I had some free time at a medical conference in Berlin, so I walked up to the Wall and picked up a piece to bring home. The five-inch piece of stone, which sits in my study, symbolizes to me how freedom eventually defeated oppression. That notion holds a special resonance for me because my grandfather, Leo Didur, immigrated to the U.S. from the Ukraine more than a century ago, moving from a country that would fall under an oppressive regime to one founded on the enlightened principle of democracy. But more specifically, that rock reminds me that the simplest ideas, even if completely misguided, lie at the heart of the biggest efforts. The Soviet Union erected an actual, miles-long wall to prevent East Berlin's residents from getting to the other side—lest they learn about the appeals of a democratic West Germany and want to migrate.

I once thought of that rock while cruising at an altitude of 30,000 feet. I'd been pondering some tough problems with clients, and I realized we often build the same sorts of impediments in the corporate world. We don't hold back entire populations from freedom, but we do box in our employees and our internal communities with rigid processes and procedures. We protect ourselves from the future by hanging on to the past. It just feels safer that way.

I was preoccupied with my thoughts, so the flight attendant politely nudged me and placed a cup of peanuts on my tray. I went back into a sort of contemplation I'd often had since writing *PreCommerce*. In the years since, I visited hundreds of Fortune 1000 companies. Even in this case, I was just returning from a few days with brilliant executives from one of the world's top companies. I'd discussed how they can use digital media and technology to transform their companies, divisions and brands. The class was energizing, and I learned as much from them as they did from me. But something didn't sit right. Back on the plane and exhausted, I tried to figure it out. While other passengers around me watched "Argo" or played blackjack on their laptops to pass the time, I turned this puzzle around in my head.

Something in my mind harkened back to my days at Dell. Back in 2008, I'd put together a new customer-response policy for the company and sent it to Michael Dell. He called me back soon after getting it. Looks good, he told me, only one problem—you forgot the decimal point between the "2" and the "4." I'd proposed a 24-hour response policy; Michael wanted his company to respond much more quickly. He said it with a semi-laugh, but he had a serious point—an eye-opening one for me. I realized I should've started at zero hours and worked my way to the right response time, rather than start at 24 hours and hope I could gain consensus. My internal barriers, in my brain, prevented me from innovating faster. I had become my own Berlin Wall.

I chuckled a bit at the memory, picking a peanut or two, but my mind was already processing the next step. I'd entered what my wife and daughters call "Bob World." They usually have to wave their hands to snap me out of it. The flight attendant must have seen I was in Bob World when I ordered a Diet Coke, because I didn't recall ordering it. My focus had already drifted back well before my Dell days, to my work at Novartis and then-CEO Dr. Dan Vasella.

Dr. Vasella would talk with great passion about how Novartis would help eradicate disease in developing countries, often in partnership with governments. He didn't talk about whether or not the company might accomplish this; he talked with certainty about how we would solve previously insurmountable problems. With him at the helm, we would go as far as possible to help others and improve society—period, full stop. He envisioned malarial drugs such as Coartem saving millions of lives, and still other pharmaceuticals driving away leprosy, tuberculosis and the other scourges of the developing world.

Dr. Vasella could only see how to scale walls and make a difference. He refused to hear about delays.

I grabbed a couple more peanuts and thought about a pair of similarly driven and inspirational leaders at Rhone-Poulenc Rorer—CEO Rob Cawthorn, and President Michel de Rosen. Back in 1994, Jim Weiss and I were working with our colleagues there to get Taxotere approved by the FDA. It would eventually become one of the world's greatest cancer drugs, but it almost didn't make it to market. The Oncologic Drugs Advisory Committee at the FDA had summarily rejected it, devastating the team that had put so much time and effort into something we knew to be a revolutionary treatment. Morale couldn't have been much lower, but rather than console us or cheerlead, Cawthorn and de Rosen simply discussed what our plan would be to gain approval the following year. In their minds, the rejection was no more than an unfortunate speed bump. The vision never changed, and hundreds of thousands of people with cancer have since benefitted.

Great leaders see opportunities. They never see barriers; they visualize solutions. And they know how to unlock their personal innovation.

And on that plane, I slowly started to draw some connections. Great leaders see opportunities. They never see barriers; they visualize solutions. And they know how to unlock their personal innovation—the same skill I'd shared with the executives with whom I'd just met. Still, something else much bigger gnawed at me. Still floating in Bob World, I started to consider how my experience with digital media changed as, over the years, I shifted from the pharmaceutical industry to Dell and the sizzling pace of the high-tech world. Each of the brilliant executives I worked with approach innovation in different ways, but they all had a common ability to unlock it within themselves and their teams. We each have to tap into that common thread of leadership, but we also have to rely on our own strengths.

I was stumped. If consumers could rapidly change the way they consume media, and if startups could create new technologies at breakneck speed, why couldn't the Fortune 1000 companies transform with the speed necessary to optimize their use of digital media and build an advantage with it. And an avalanche of questions came pouring down.

Why do companies or organizations take forever to change? Why does most innovation occur in small teams? Why do companies make it so hard for innovators to evolve products, services and companies? Basically, why can one person make such a big difference, yet 100,000 people in a Fortune 500 company hold each other back?

WE HAVE SEEN THE ENEMY, AND IT IS CROWDSENSING

The flight attendant returned with the Diet Coke I'd forgotten and placed it beside my peanuts. Like the sharp physical blow that snaps a meditating monk into enlightenment, her simple act of setting down the Diet Coke jolted me to my answer. Of course the largest barrier to innovation is our failure to unlock our individual creativity—that was a no-brainer. But I realized then and there that the largest barrier to innovation at a company is actually erected by all of us, collectively. In a twisted way, we actually crowdsource the walls we build against organizational innovation.

If crowdsourcing from the marketplace can lead to big ideas, 'crowdsensing' within an organization works equally hard to hold us back.

I took a sip of my drink and put it into words: "If crowdsourcing from the marketplace can lead to big ideas, 'crowdsensing' within an organization works equally hard to hold us back. Crowds wield tremendous power, both for and against our goals."

A crowdsensing company rests on inertia rather than driving in new directions. Corporate habits rebel against new ideas that could change how we think about and conduct our business, and we rarely realize it. Think about the reception your company gives to new ideas. I used to think innovation was a lonely business; now I feared it was downright solitary. Your new idea represents an abnormality, and the crowd abhors change. Our habits drive us, and routine behavior becomes our crutch. This is all fine and dandy if you don't need to change, but it's hard to imagine any scenario in which change doesn't eventually occur.

AN ANTIDOTE FOR CROWDSENSING

We don't break out of this corporate, crowdsensed rut by focusing on the customer, starting a new customer-experience campaign or gathering insights from your customers on a regular basis. That's how companies agree to get new inputs, but they derive from the same failed way of thinking. No, rather than focusing on the customer, we need to *always* put ourselves in the minds of the customer—as if we were them. To someone from the outside just walking into our conference room, the tone and content of our internal conversation should make our visitor assume that some of the people there are customers, not employees. We don't assume we know the optimal solution, because more often than not our customers do. We need to think of the marketplace as if the customer no longer needs us. We need them, so we will figure out what we have to do to sustain our relationship.

This mindset flips all our models upside down. We have no sacred cows, except the ideas and products our customers, the bosses, make sacrosanct. They will give the thumbs up or down on how we operate and let us know in real time. Advertising, CRM, search, direct marketing, communications and other disciplines will become more relevant to our customer, or disappear entirely. We have to let go of what we see as control, and we have to let go of the old media models whose value is rapidly deteriorating.

Our jobs will necessarily evolve, as well. Technology has developed to the point at which our customers can become self-sufficient—from how they buy our products, how they find their next employers and how they evaluate the reputation and the relevance of our company.

THE END OF GROUPTHINK

The macro facts we like to tell ourselves aren't unique. Every one of our competitors have the same information. But we gather research and bring in consultants to tell us about the growth rate of mobile in China and e-commerce forecasts for North America. I like to call those sessions "corporate daycare." A company gathers all of its executives in one place, and then occupies them in a manner that's more fun than informative. If a consultant feeds them enough new facts, they might get hired again—never mind that another consultant just gave the same information to the archrival. Meanwhile, those who attend these classes know, deep down, that they could've found any of this insight with a little basic homework. They just spent eight hours at corporate daycare, when instead they could've discussed customer feedback that hints at major shifts in the way we market, sell, service and operate.

You see, innovators operate with a mix of fear, restlessness and general paranoia. They're never satisfied, and a daylong course of corporate daycare would drive them nuts. If it doesn't drive you nuts, perhaps you're too complacent. The quest to be the best doesn't have an exit ramp, but that's not to say we all have to be Steve Jobs. We just need to know how to learn from experience and do so at a pace that keeps up with or, even better, slightly surpasses the innovation of the market itself.

But groupthink and crowdsensing slow our pace. When our colleagues within the company too heavily influence our thinking, we miss trends because we haven't put our customers' feedback into practice. Jobs famously said he didn't need to do research because he already knew what people wanted. It sounded arrogant, but I would argue that it was actually amazingly perceptive. He was so ingeniously innovative for deceptively simple reasons. *He thought like a customer. He created the experience that he knew customers would want. And he marketed and sold his products in the way consumers wanted to be marketed and sold to.*

In his mind, Jobs *was* the customer. No wonder he disliked committees, bureaucracy and formal market research—in our daily lives as consumers, don't we all?

REJUVENATE YOUR THINKING

Most of us will resist change, at first. We'll keep reading the same reports and secondary research our competitors have. We'll do the same primary research using the same methodology we've employed for the past decade. We'll hold on tight to the models we learned in business school. And ultimately, our thinking will grow more rigid, not less. Intellectually, we'll not be aging well. But unlike the physical aging of our body, we can become young again if we deliberately choose to learn differently, evolve our models and commit ourselves to understanding how the marketplace is truly changing.

Customers have unlocked the ability to get what they need and influence their communities, and they can do it far faster than the average company. Going forward, progressive companies will learn how to co-build, co-service, co-brand and co-support with customers to create value for the audience and the company. We will be participating in a form of open-source innovation, with the company and customer as part of the same, free-flowing organization.

> In the Storytizing world, our corporate and individual narratives don't combine into a singular plot. They all weave into a grand tale—one where each unique strand only adds more richness, color and inspiration to a story we all tell together.

As I ate my final few peanuts and finished the last of my Diet Coke, I felt revived by this notion of an open-source, free-flowing organization that counts both the company and the customer as members in equal standing. I'd come to realize that this was the new foundation for innovation and success in today's business environment. Our companies, employees and customers are all part of a singular narrative, yet we need to ensure we don't let it limit us. We can crowdsource without falling into crowdsense. We can rely on our collective knowledge without stunting progress via groupthink.

In the Storytizing world, our corporate and individual narratives don't combine into a singular plot. They all weave into a grand tale—one where each unique strand only adds more richness, color and inspiration to a story we all tell together.

THE STORY OF MALCOLM LLOYD

By Jeff Arnold, who changes how we do business.
In 1998, he founded WebMD and changed how we find health information.
He rebuilt HowStuffWorks.com and changed how we use search effectively.
He is now transforming how we experience health and wellness as Chairman and
CEO of Sharecare and how we think of hospitality as Chairman of Forbes Travel Guide.

In the spirit of Storytizing, I wanted to share the unique journey of an incredibly smart, charismatic, out-of-the box thinker named Malcolm Lloyd. I met Malcolm in 2012, as he was building his spirits company, Double Cross, into a well-known and enviable luxury brand. I was struck immediately by how he was affecting change in one industry by leveraging the extensive training and education he received in another.

Malcolm studied biomedical engineering at Johns Hopkins University and earned his Doctor of Medicine from Dartmouth. His original plan was orthopedic surgery, but he realized after graduating from Dartmouth that he was, at his core, an entrepreneur. He changed course and ran his own business in the medical-device sector until his godfather inspired him to take a look at the spirits industry. There, Malcolm's vision and passion came into focus: He would create a next-generation, ultra-premium vodka brand.

No surprise to anyone who knew him, Malcolm approached this opportunity with surgical precision, applying the principles of clinical trials to come up with the perfect formula. He worked with a partner – his godfather and mentor Dr. Jan Krak, himself a Slovakian master distiller – to create a grain-based spirit marked by its smooth flavor and distinctively engraved bottle. Double Cross Vodka hit shelves in September 2008 at the height of the global financial crisis.

Unfazed by the uncertain market, Malcolm remained committed to establishing a luxury brand that would elevate the vodka category. His inventive thinking was not only in the making of the product but extended into the development of unexpected marketing and distribution partnerships, which in turn enabled him to scale quickly when most new spirit brands were failing. Double Cross would earn a 95-point designation from *Wine Enthusiast*, and Goldman Sachs honored Malcolm for his achievements by naming him one of the 100 Most Innovative Entrepreneurs.

Whenever we discussed business or brainstormed the next big idea, Malcolm inspired me to apply different lenses and filters to see what others did not. Unfortunately, I don't have the opportunity to continue these thought provoking conversations with Malcolm. He died tragically in a car accident in 2014. However, his legacy and passion lives on in those of us he touched. Though Malcolm's story was way too short, it is rooted in innovation, risk-taking, opportunism, impact and, most importantly, connecting the seemingly disparate dots to change an established industry with new and improved ways of thinking.

Over the next three
to five years, technology advances
and their impact on cost will fuel
the most rapid pace of innovation
we've ever seen in our lives.
Here is a great perspective
from one of the leaders
in identifying and incubating
the world's next companies.

WHY INNOVATION WILL ACCELERATE IN A STORYTIZING WORLD

By Joshua Baer

Josh likes to say he helps people quit their jobs and become entrepreneurs at Capital Factory, Austin's center of gravity for entrepreneurs. He founded his first startup in 1996 in his college dormitory at Carnegie Mellon University. He was recently recognized as a Henry Crown Fellow and Braddock Scholar at the Aspen Institute, a member of the National Committee on U.S.-China Relations Young Leaders Forum, and an Eisenhower Fellow.

Technology entrepreneurship is flourishing because the capital requirements in almost every category are trending towards zero. It used to cost $5 million to start a company and validate whether the business works. You used to need $1 million for hardware, $1 million for software, $1 million for database, $1 million for advertising and $1 million for people – and that funding was limited to the well-educated and well-connected few who had access to venture capital. Over the past 20 years, cloud computing, open source software, social media, outsourcing and crowdfunding have virtually eliminated all of those costs for many types of businesses.

CLOUD COMPUTING has enabled small startups to avoid the upfront costs of buying servers and equipment and the complexity (some might say futility) of trying to predict usage accurately. In the past, a new company would have to try and predict how much demand there would be at launch and buy enough servers ahead of time to handle it. Growth has to be planned, ordered and installed months in advance. Buy too little and their big launch is a dud. Buy too much and they waste a lot of money. Today, they just buy the smallest amount at the beginning and add more capacity as needed, without having to plan ahead. This saves lots of money and eliminates the need to plan precisely for capacity. That's $1 million saved on hardware.

OPEN SOURCE SOFTWARE has replaced most of the core systems we used to pay for. When I got involved with computers in the 1980s, most open source software wasn't as reliable or up-to-date as commercial software. Today, open-source software is the standard and is often the most reliable. That's $2 million saved on software and database.

MEDIA used to be controlled by a small number of companies that operated television and news. Today, some media is controlled by the masses through social media and crowdfunding. Many businesses have attracted millions of customers without spending any money on ads. That's $1 million saved on advertising.

OUTSOURCING has turned people into objects in the cloud, with the same benefits. Spin up or spin down human resources the same way you spin up or spin down servers. Hire people on the other side of the world and pay them by the month, by the hour, or by the word. That's $1 million saved on people.

That's it! All our costs are gone. Now it's free. You just have to have a good idea and be resourceful, and you can create the next Facebook.

ABOUT THE AUTHOR

Bob Pearson is Senior Advisor of W2O Group, an independent network of digital communications and marketing companies.

He is an author, frequent speaker and blogger on digital marketing, as well as an adjunct professor at Syracuse University, The University of Texas McCombs School and a guest lecturer at the U.S. State Department's Marketing College. He has written two books (*PreCommerce* and *Storytizing*) based on key learnings from the firm's work with innovative companies and individuals. Bob's third book, *Countering Hate*, co-authored with Haroon K. Ullah, explores how bias, hate and extremism forms, how we can counter it and what we can learn from extremist groups. He is currently working on a fourth book with Haroon (*Web War III: The Content Wars*) and a fifth with Kip Knight & Ed Tazzia on marketing.

Prior to W2O Group, Bob worked as VP of Communities and Conversations at Dell to develop the Fortune 500's first global social media function—an industry-leading approach to the use of social media, as highlighted in the best seller, *GroundSwell*. Before Dell, Bob was Head of Global Corporate Communications and Head of Global Pharma Communications at Novartis Pharmaceuticals in Basel, Switzerland, where he served on the Pharma Executive Committee and he held the role of Vice President of Media and Public Affairs for Rhone-Poulenc Rorer (now Sanofi).

Bob serves as an advisor and investor in many capacities. Highlights include: serving as an original member of the P&G digital advisory board; being appointed by the Governor of Texas to serve as chair and vice chair of the emerging technology fund for the State of Texas (more than $400MM invested); and currently serving on the boards of Vetted. org, The Advertising Research Foundation, Genprex, Inc. and as interim CEO of the MedicAlert Foundation, as well as acting as an advisor for the University of Texas Center for Global Business. Bob resides in Austin, Texas with his wife Donna.

INDEX

CPSIA information can be obtained
at www.ICGtesting.com
Printed in the USA
LVHW082109210720
661232LV00012B/366/J